Flying Feathers

A Farce

Derek Benfield

A Samuel French Acting Edition

Founded 1830

SAMUELFRENCH-LONDON.CO.UK
SAMUELFRENCH.COM

Copyright © 1987 by Derek Benfield
All Rights Reserved

FLYING FEATHERS is fully protected under the copyright laws of the British Commonwealth, including Canada, the United States of America, and all other countries of the Copyright Union. All rights, including professional and amateur stage productions, recitation, lecturing, public reading, motion picture, radio broadcasting, television and the rights of translation into foreign languages are strictly reserved.

ISBN 978-0-573-01657-8

www.samuelfrench-london.co.uk

www.samuelfrench.com

FOR AMATEUR PRODUCTION ENQUIRIES

UNITED KINGDOM AND WORLD
EXCLUDING NORTH AMERICA

plays@SamuelFrench-London.co.uk

020 7255 4302/01

Each title is subject to availability from Samuel French,
depending upon country of performance.

CAUTION: Professional and amateur producers are hereby warned that *FLYING FEATHERS* is subject to a licensing fee. Publication of this play does not imply availability for performance. Both amateurs and professionals considering a production are strongly advised to apply to the appropriate agent before starting rehearsals, advertising, or booking a theatre. A licensing fee must be paid whether the title is presented for charity or gain and whether or not admission is charged.

The professional rights in this play are controlled by Lemon Unna & Durbridge, Summit House, 170 Finchley Road, London, NW3 6BP.

No one shall make any changes in this title for the purpose of production. No part of this book may be reproduced, stored in a retrieval system, or transmitted in any form, by any means, now known or yet to be invented, including mechanical, electronic, photocopying, recording, videotaping, or otherwise, without the prior written permission of the publisher. No one shall upload this title, or part of this title, to any social media websites.

The right of Derek Benfield to be identified as author of this work has been asserted by him in accordance with Section 77 of the Copyright, Designs and Patents Act 1988

FLYING FEATHERS

First presented by Helmut Siderits at the Kleine Komödie Theater, Vienna, on September 5th, 1987, with the following cast of characters:

Sarah Potterton	Trude Marlen
Henry Potterton	Walter Scheuer
Polly	Helga Hummel
Debbie	Claudia Androsch
Nora Winthrop	Maria Perschy
Sally	Verena Felden
Jackie	Christine Saginth
Roger Featherstone	Viktor Couzyn
Mr Tunnicliffe	Andreas Steppan
A Visitor	Walter Scheuer

The play directed by **Helmut Siderits**
German translation by **Wolfgang Spier**
Setting by **Wolfgang Müller-Karbach**

The play takes place in a peaceful old house in the depths of the country

ACT I   An afternoon in Spring

ACT II
  Scene 1   A few minutes later
  Scene 2   A little later

Time - the present

ACT I

A delightful, peaceful, oak-beamed house in the country. Possibly once an old mill. No doubt a trout stream in the garden. It is a pleasant spring afternoon and the sun is shining

There are four entrances: an archway URC *leading to the front door; french windows* UC *leading out on to a paved patio where there is an abundance of potted plants; a larger archway* UL*; and a door* DR*. There is also a door into a cupboard* DL*.* R *is a bow window with a padded window-seat. Amongst the heavy, ornate furniture is a sofa* RC *with a small table* L *of it on which is a telephone and a desk diary; a drinks cupboard below the archway* L*, with a chair next to it; a corner table* UL *with a lamp on it; a bookcase against the wall above the window-seat; a hall-stand in the passage* UR*; an oak chest outside the archway* UL*; and a stool below the cupboard door* DL*. On the walls are a mirror and various oil paintings of country scenes and animal life. Throughout the play "archway" refers to the archway* UL

Sarah, a slight, gentle woman in her fifties, comes apprehensively in from the front door. She is laden with suitcases, carrier bags and fishing rods. She wears a hat.

Sarah looks about, uncertainly, and wanders to C*, teetering a little under her burden. Suddenly, outside the bow window a cow moos loudly. Sarah jumps, dropping the luggage in an untidy heap*

Sarah Aaaaah!

She runs back to call to somebody outside

(*Off*) Henry! (*Then a little more sharply*) Henry! Quickly!
Henry (*off*) All right! Hang on! I'm coming!

Sarah staggers back into the room, looking nervously towards the bow window through which she has heard the cow

Henry strides in. He is a pleasant, middle-aged man with the confident, relaxed air of a Chief Constable. Unlike Sarah, he carries no luggage

Whatever's the matter?
Sarah (*urgently*) Look out there! (*She points to the bow window*)

Henry trots across to the window, Sarah following close behind him like a shadow. He peers out, anxiously

See?

Henry What?
Sarah Cows!
Henry (*giving her a baleful look*) Cows? Is that all? I thought you were being murdered. (*He wanders away below the sofa, looking about*)
Sarah (*grumbling as she follows him*) Well, they never said there'd be cows! I hope *I'm* not expected to milk them.
Henry Don't be ridiculous. They'll have people for that. People in boots.
Sarah They never said anything about livestock. You're sure this *is* Bernard's house?
Henry Of course it's Bernard's house! It's the address in Mr Tunnicliffe's letter.
Sarah Who's Mr Tunnicliffe?
Henry (*trying to be patient*) The solicitor, Sarah. Of Tunnicliffe, Tunnicliffe, Tipthorpe and Tunnicliffe. (*He looks around, enthusiastically*) H'm. Seems a very nice place. Very peaceful.
Sarah Except for the cows ...
Henry Just the spot for a busy man like me to unwind.
Sarah You're not here to unwind, Henry. You're here to sort out Bernard's affairs.
Henry There'll still be time for a little fishing. (*He moves away and sees the untidy pile of luggage*) Did *you* leave these here?
Sarah (*a little sheepish*) Yes—when I heard the cows.
Henry Well, you didn't have to throw them about. You're not working for the Post Office. (*He tidies the luggage a little*)
Sarah (*perching on the sofa, thoughtfully*) Poor Bernard. Fancy dying in the Orkneys. I can't think why he did it ...
Henry I don't suppose he had much choice. When they call your number, it's no good arguing. You've just got to shout "Bingo" and start climbing.
Sarah Climbing?
Henry Up the stairs.

She still looks blank

To the Pearly Gates! (*He points towards heaven*)
Sarah Don't be silly. He fell off his tractor.
Henry That doesn't mean he can't go to heaven.
Sarah I can't think what he was doing on a tractor in the first place. Bernard couldn't even drive a motor car. And I'm surprised at you, Henry. You should have *known* he was going to die.
Henry How could I possibly know that? He was in Scotland.
Sarah But you and Bernard are twins. I thought twins always knew what was going to happen to one another.
Henry Bernard and I may have looked alike, but we were miles apart in other respects.
Sarah Yes. I can't see *you* going off to live on a religious commune in the Orkneys. (*She chuckles at the thought*)

Act I   3

Henry looks at her, coldly and wanders away L

Henry We all have different ways of serving the community. Bernard's was through prayer; mine is through the Police Force. (*He has discovered the drinks cupboard*) Ah! That's more like it. I could do with a drink after that drive. Is this one of your drinking days?

Sarah cheers up at once

Sarah
Henry } (*nodding, together*) Yes!

Henry I don't know why I asked. (*He starts to pour a whisky and a sherry*)
Sarah Do you think we should?
Henry Why not?
Sarah It belongs to Bernard.
Henry Well, it's not much use to *him* now!

There is a loud blast on a whistle from off L

Sarah Aaah! (*She jumps up, nervously,* L *of the sofa*) What was that?
Henry Only someone blowing a whistle.
Sarah Yes, Henry. But *who*?
Henry Boy Scouts, probably. You always find them in the woods at this time of the year.
Sarah Really? *I've* never noticed. It gave me quite a shock...
Henry (*crossing to her with their drinks*) You'll feel better when you've had a drink.

Sarah takes her drink

Well, here's to... brother Bernard!
Sarah *Absent* brother Bernard...

They drink, solemnly. Sarah drifts back towards the bow window

I can't think why he never said there were cows... (*She turns to look at Henry*) You know I still can't believe that he's dead. It wouldn't surprise me if he suddenly walked in through that door.

But it is Polly who walks in through the door DR. *She is an extremely pretty young lady. She crosses to* C *and comes face-to-face with Henry*

Polly Ooh! I didn't know anyone was here.
Henry Just arrived.
Polly Have you got a booking?
Henry (*blankly*) I beg your pardon?
Polly Are you expected?
Henry Er—no, not exactly, but——
Polly Well, it's no good just turning up on the off-chance. I don't suppose anyone's free.
Sarah Henry—what's she talking about?

Polly turns and sees Sarah for the first time. She giggles

Polly She doesn't belong to *you*, does she?
Henry Good Lord, no! She's my sister.
Polly Funny place to bring your sister! Look, I can't stop, love. I'm already late for the bank manager. Didn't you hear the whistle?
Sarah Yes—Boy Scouts!
Polly (*puzzled*) No—Mrs Winthrop! (*To Henry*) I'll tell her you're here. Perhaps *she* can see to you.

She goes out through the archway

Henry and Sarah are left totally dismayed

Henry Fancy going to see your bank manager dressed like that.
Sarah Do you suppose she's one of the staff? A maid or something?
Henry I've never seen a maid looking like that!
Sarah And who's Mrs Winthrop?
Henry No idea. Bernard left old Mrs Parker in charge.
Sarah I can't think why we're not expected ...
Henry Well, they didn't know we were coming, did they?
Sarah I told you to telephone them first. (*She looks out of the window*) I don't like the look of those cows one bit ...

Debbie comes in from the door DR. *Another very pretty girl. She crosses to* C *and comes face-to-face with Henry. She smiles a nice, welcoming smile*

Debbie Ah—hullo! Are you waiting for *me*?
Henry Er—no. I don't think so.
Debbie I thought perhaps you were Mr Curtis.
Henry Curtis? No. I'm Potterton.
Debbie Oh. I don't think we're expecting a Potterton.
Henry Are you Mrs Winthrop?
Debbie (*laughing*) No, of course not! I'm just one of her girls.
Henry Girls?
Debbie Can't you tell?
Henry How many of you are there?
Debbie Only four at the moment.
Henry All working for Mrs Winthrop?
Debbie Yes.
Henry Good Lord ...
Debbie (*crossing below him*) Now, who's expecting *you*, I wonder ...
Henry Ah—well, you see—as a matter of fact——
Debbie (*turning*) Oh, of course! It'll be Jackie. Hers hasn't turned up yet. I'll tell her you're here. (*She sees Sarah*) And who are *you*?
Sarah I'm his sister.
Debbie Come to hold his hand, have you?

She giggles, and goes out through the archway

Sarah I never thought Bernard would employ girls looking like that.
Henry Neither did I! I can't think why he went off to the Orkneys. (*He chuckles, gazing after Debbie*)

Act I

Sarah You'll have to speak to them.
Henry (*enthusiastically*) Yes, I certainly will! (*He starts to go*)
Sarah Henry . . .!

Henry stops and hastily assumes a more sober mien

Henry I mean—they really shouldn't wander about dressed like that. Bad for discipline.
Sarah (*looking out of the window*) There must be five or six of them.
Henry (*surprised*) What?!
Sarah Cows. Out there.
Henry Really? (*He joins her at the window and looks out*) Good Lord . . .
Sarah It'll be a bit of a shock if I *do* have to milk them.
Henry It certainly will. They're bulls. (*He moves away to* C)

Nora Winthrop comes sailing in through the archway. She is a cheerful, enthusiastic woman, but at the moment is not too pleased at seeing intruders

Nora You can't come in here!
Henry I beg your pardon?
Nora You're not expected.
Sarah Oh, yes, we are! (*She joins Henry*)
Nora Look, dear—I know who's expected and who's not and you're not.
Henry Well, we're here.
Nora So I see. *And* helping yourselves to the drink!
Henry Well, there's no sign of tea.
Nora This isn't a café!
Henry I know that.
Nora Then I suggest you get out of here right away. If you had an appointment, I'd *know*—and you haven't—so on your bike! (*She sees their luggage*) And what's all this?
Henry Luggage.
Nora You can't leave luggage lying there!
Henry Then you'd better move it.
Nora (*outraged*) I'm not here to move luggage!
Henry Then what *are* you here for?
Nora I'm the housekeeper—Mrs Winthrop.
Henry } (*together, to each other*) { Ah—Winthrop! (*They link their little
Sarah } { fingers*)
Sarah Do you milk the cows yourself?

Henry gives her a weary look

Henry Well, Mrs Winthrop, we've had a long journey and we'd like a cup of tea.

Nora stares at them, beadily

Nora Tea? I'm far too busy to make tea.
Sarah Henry, are you going to let her talk like that?
Nora (*glancing at Sarah*) Who *is* that? You haven't brought your wife, have you, dear?

Henry Good Lord, no! She's my sister.
Nora Oh, that's all right, then. (*She takes his arm and leads him away a little*) We don't get many wives arriving here, I can tell you! (*She laughs, saucily, and squeezes his arm*) You haven't been here before, I take it, dear?
Henry No. This is my first visit. But I've heard all about it from my brother.
Nora (*delighted*) Oh, you were recommended? I *am* glad. That's how we get most of our customers. By word of mouth.
Henry (*puzzled*) Customers?
Sarah Henry—what's she talking about?
Henry Leave this to me, Sarah. I'll deal with this.

Sarah sits on the sofa with her drink, totally bewildered

We meet a lot of funny people in the Police Force. You don't become a Chief Constable without learning how to deal with funny people.
Nora (*intrigued*) Oo, you're a Chief Constable, are you?
Henry Certainly.
Nora We get all sorts here, you know. But we've never had a Chief Constable before. Oh, what a pity! That *is* a shame. But I'm afraid I just can't squeeze you in, dear. So I wonder if you'd mind moving your luggage out of my lobby?
Henry It isn't *your* lobby, as a matter of fact. It's my brother's lobby.
Nora Oh? And who's your brother?
Henry He's the owner of this house! *I'm* the owner's brother.

Nora smiles, patiently

Nora Look, if you were really the owner's brother, dear, you'd know that he doesn't live here anymore.
Henry He doesn't live *any*where anymore.
Nora Sorry?
Henry He's dead.
Nora *Dead?!*
Henry It happens to us all. He went to live on an island and work on the land, but he fell off his tractor.

Nora laughs, raucously, crossing to Sarah

Nora Couldn't have been much of a farmer if he fell off his tractor!
Henry Ah—well, he . . . he wasn't really a farmer, as a matter of fact. He was more of a vicar.

Nora turns and stares at him in surprise

Nora A *vicar?!*
Henry Well . . . a *sort* of a vicar.

Nora cannot believe her ears

Nora What on earth was he doing on a tractor?
Henry Helping with the harvest. Rather appropriate, I thought. Setting a lay example as well as a religious one.

Act I 7

Nora (*incredulously*) You mean he was praying as he drove around the field?
Henry Very probably.
Nora No wonder he fell off his tractor. (*She returns to him, piously*) On your knees in church.
Henry I beg your pardon?
Nora That's the place for praying. Not on a tractor in the middle of a field. He obviously couldn't see where he was going.
Sarah Oh, I don't know. He might not have had his eyes shut.
Nora If he was praying with his eyes open, then he deserves everything that happened to him. I bet he wasn't C of E. Sounds more like the Baptists to me. No self-respecting vicar would pray with his eyes open.
Henry Oh, I dunno. Our vicar always peeps during prayers. I've often spotted him, counting the congregation.
Nora And where did all this happen?
Henry All what happen?
Nora All this falling off tractors.
Henry Ah—Scotland.
Nora Oh, well, that's different, dear. Anything could happen up there. Land of kilts and cabers. (*She laughs*)
Henry My brother was living on a religious commune in the Orkneys. He decided to cut himself off from the rat race.
Sarah And now he's cut himself off permanently . . .
Nora You don't expect me to believe all this, do you? (*Reasonably*) Look, dear—I'm a very busy woman and you haven't got a booking, so would you please go? (*She tries to pull him towards the front door*)
Henry Just a minute, Mrs Winthrop. If you're the housekeeper here, what happened to old Mrs Parker?
Nora Oh, she left three months ago. (*Then, apprehensively*) You . . . you've *heard* of Mrs Parker, then?
Henry Of course we've heard of her. She was with Bernard for years.
Sarah Yes—years!

Nora looks from one to the other, aghast

Nora Oh, my God . . .! You really *are* his brother and sister!
Henry You should never doubt the word of a Chief Constable. (*He peers into her face as if she was a suspect*) So, Mrs Winthrop—how did *you* come to get the job here? Not through my brother because he was in the Orkneys.
Nora Oh, no—it was all arranged by Mrs Parker. She took me on when she left. I've got very good references!
Henry I should jolly well hope so! I can safely assume then that you've been running this house exactly the way my brother would have wished?
Nora (*nervously*) Oh—oh, yes! Of course! Oh, my God . . .!
Henry Is anything the matter, Mrs Winthrop?
Nora Er—no—no, nothing at all!
Henry You seem rather perturbed.

Nora No, no—I'm fine! But you should have let us know that you were coming——
Sarah That's what *I* told him . . . (*She gives Henry a look*)
Nora Then we could have had everything ready for you. (*She takes out a whistle, goes to the archway and blows two shrill blasts*)

Henry and Sarah look astonished

Sarah You see, Henry? It wasn't Boy Scouts at all.
Henry (*as Nora returns*) Is the house on fire?
Nora Oh, no! No! Of course not! No! Oh, my God . . .! (*She marches across to the door* DR *and blows two more blasts on her whistle*)

Henry watches in wonder

Sarah (*thoughtfully*) I don't mind feeding pigs, but milking's quite another matter . . .
Henry Milking the pigs?
Sarah The cows! You see, I've had no experience.
Henry Can't be very difficult. You'll soon get the hang of it. (*To Nora, who is on her way again*) And where are *you* going?
Nora (*crossing to* C) I just want a word with the staff.

Polly comes running in through the archway. She is now only half-dressed

Henry and Sarah gaze at her in surprise

Polly What are you blowing the whistle for? It can't be time yet!
Nora (*going to Polly, quickly*) Why are you dressed like that?
Polly What?
Nora You should be outside seeing to the pigs!
Polly What are you talking about?
Nora (*grimly*) I'd like you to see to the pigs, Polly.
Polly I'm not messing about with them!
Nora (*to Henry*) She's supposed to be seeing to the pigs.
Henry Dressed like that?
Nora (*hissing at Polly*) Go and take those clothes off!
Polly That's what I *was* doing when you rang the bell. (*To Henry*) I don't know what's got into her today. She's not usually like this.
Nora Go and see to the pigs, Polly!
Polly I can't think what you're making such a fuss about. (*Crossing to Henry*) Has she fixed you up all right, dear? (*To Nora*) We didn't know he was coming, did we?
Nora No, we didn't . . .!
Polly (*to Henry, sweetly*) Next time don't forget to telephone and make an appointment, love.
Henry Appointment?!
Polly Now don't be shy. We all know what you're here for.
Henry Well, I was rather hoping for cucumber sandwiches.
Polly (*giggling*) Don't tell me *that*'s all you want!
Nora The pigs, Polly!!

Act I

Henry Just a minute, Mrs Winthrop. (*To Polly*) Now look here—my sister and I have had a very long journey——
Sarah Yes—*very* long...

Henry gives her a look before continuing

Henry So before you see to the pigs, I'd be grateful if you'd go and slip into flat shoes, plain dress, white apron, little hat and return here with a pot of tea, cucumber sandwiches and a piece of cake on a silver salver.
Polly All right, dear—whatever turns you on.

Nora is appalled. She hastily grabs Polly's arm and moves her away from Henry

Nora Polly! Go and do what the *Chief Constable* says!
Polly What?
Nora Yes! This gentleman is a *Chief Constable*!
Polly A copper? (*Delighted*) Ooooh! We've never had one of them before. But what about the bank manager?
Nora You can see the bank manager tomorrow!
Polly But he's here! Now!
Nora Well, get rid of him!
Henry I've never had a bank manager who came to visit *me*. I always had to make an appointment.
Polly He *had*!
Nora (*to Henry*) He's very worried about her overdraft. She ignores his letters, you see. So he had to come here to find her.
Henry And is he satisfied now?
Polly No—not yet! (*She giggles*)

Nora urges Polly on her way, desperately

Nora Look—something unexpected has cropped up! So tell the bank manager to go away and come again another day!
Polly He won't like it.
Nora Never mind. Get rid of him!
Polly Oh, all right. But he's not going to be pleased. (*To Henry*) A Chief Constable, eh? Well, I hope you've brought your truncheon with you!

She goes out through the archway, with a saucy smile

Nora is appalled. She goes to Henry, concerned

Nora I do hope your sandwiches turn out all right. She's not very good with a cucumber.
Sarah (*deep in thought*) I suppose I could always go down to the church and practise on the bell ropes...

Debbie returns through the archway

Debbie I've had a word with Jackie. She says if you haven't got a booking *she* can fit you in.
Henry I beg your pardon?

Nora (*crossing to Debbie, urgently*) Debbie! Why are you dressed like that? What *will* the Chief Constable think?
Debbie A copper? Oo, lovely!
Nora You're supposed to be cleaning the cow-shed.
Debbie Doing what?
Nora It's Wednesday! You always clean the cow-shed on Wednesday!
Debbie What?
Henry She's not exactly dressed for cleaning the cow-shed.
Nora Debbie—go and change!
Debbie But what about Mr Curtis?
Nora Send him home! And go and change into the clothes you usually wear for cleaning the cow-shed! (*She pushes Debbie*)
Debbie (*crossing to the door* DR) I don't know what's got into you today...
Nora The cow-shed!
Debbie The cow-shed...

She goes out DR

Embarrassed, Nora tries to laugh it off

Nora I have to be so firm with them sometimes.
Henry Who's Mr Curtis?
Nora Oh—er—he's in insurance. And he's such a nuisance. Simply won't take no for an answer from my girls.
Sarah I'm not surprised...

Sally comes in from the archway, wrapped in a flimsy dressing-gown. Yet another pretty girl. She goes to Nora

Sally Why did you go and blow the whistle, Mrs Winthrop? I'd only just got my clothes off.

Henry and Sarah react, puzzled. Nora panics

Nora Well, go and put them on again!
Sally (*surprised*) Pardon?
Henry (*to Nora*) Is this *another* of your girls?
Nora Oh—er—yes. This is Sally. She was just going to have a shower when I blew the whistle.
Sally No, I wasn't—I was just going to——
Nora Go and get dressed!

Jackies comes in through the archway, also half-dressed. Another one!

Jackie I wish you'd stop blowing that whistle, Mrs Winthrop. I thought the police were here.
Nora They are!

Sarah is unable to believe her eyes

Sarah *Another* girl?
Henry This place is just like the *Folies Bergère*.
Nora (*desperately gracious*) This is Jackie.

Act I

Henry How do you do, Jackie.
Jackie (*crossing to Henry*) Are you the one without a booking?
Henry (*puzzled*) Sorry?

Nora intervenes, hastily

Nora Jackie! The Chief Constable has arrived unexpectedly, and so——
Jackie (*to Henry*) Well, don't you worry, love. My chap hasn't turned up so I'm free at the moment. (*She takes his arm*)
Henry Er—I don't——
Nora Her cousin! (*She drags Jackie away from Henry and tries to hide her behind her back*)
Jackie What?
Nora Her cousin was coming to take her out to tea.
Jackie What are you talking about?
Nora So now she's free if you'd like to see her potato harvester.
Sally See her what?

Sally and Jackie look at each other and giggle

Jackie What's she on about?
Sally I dunno. I think she's gone mad ...
Henry Well, that's very kind of you, Jackie. Very kind. But perhaps I'll look at it some other time. I don't want to keep you away from your work, do I?
Nora Right, then, girls! You two go and get your clothes on. What will the Chief Constable and his sister think of you? You should be feeding the chickens by now.
Sally Feeding the chickens?

Jackie and Sally giggle together and race off again, making chicken noises as they go through the archway

Henry crosses, thoughtfully, to put his empty glass back on the drinks cupboard

Henry How many of these girls have you got working for you?
Nora Only four at the moment. It's a quiet time of the year.
Henry Isn't it rather unusual to have such pretty girls working on the land?
Nora Yes. I suppose it is, really.
Henry Do you get them locally?
Nora Oh, yes. I just ring up the Job Centre and round they come.
Henry Hardly *dressed* for farm work, though, are they? I'd have thought they'd be wearing big sweaters and boots.
Sarah Yes, if they go out into the fields dressed like that *any*thing could happen ...

Nora gives her a baleful look

Henry Haven't you got any *men* working for you?

Nora laughs, finding this amusing in spite of everything

Nora Not likely!
Henry But what about the harvest?

Nora had not thought about the harvest

Nora What harvest? Oh—yes—I suppose there's bound to be that.
Henry And harvesting is very heavy work. Do you think girls like that will be able to manage?
Nora Oh, yes. All my girls are very good in the hay.

Polly returns

Polly I'm afraid there's a bit of a problem!
Nora Don't tell me you haven't got rid of him?
Polly Who?
Nora The bank manager!
Polly Give us a chance. I'm doing the sandwiches first.
Henry I thought I asked you to change?
Polly Well, I can't find any cucumbers. Would cheese and chutney do?
Henry (*wearily*) Never mind. It doesn't matter. We'll save ourselves for supper. Come along, Sarah. Let's go and unpack.
Polly Unpack? You're not *staying*, are you?
Henry Of course we're staying.
Polly What? (*She looks at Nora*)
Nora Of course they're staying.
Henry So perhaps you'd be good enough to show us to our rooms.
Nora Yes, Polly. Show the Chief Constable and his sister to the two rooms at the back. (*Then, quietly*) And then go and get rid of the bank manager!
Polly Oh, all right . . .
Nora And tell the girls to tidy up the other rooms. Make sure there's nobody lying about!
Henry What?
Nora Nothing lying about! We'll soon have you both settled in, Chief Constable. Polly—the luggage!

Reluctantly, Polly goes to get some of the luggage

Polly (*grumbling*) You'd think I was a bleedin' porter . . .
Nora (*to Henry*) Now—you'll be in Oak—(*to Sarah*)—and you'll be in Ash.
Sarah I'm not sleeping out in the garden!
Henry (*to Nora*) What are you talking about?
Nora All the rooms are named after trees. I think that's rather nice, don't you? Makes you feel you're in the country.
Henry We *are* in the country. Was that my brother's idea?
Nora I suppose it must have been.
Henry No wonder he went to live on an island.

Polly is on her way with some of the luggage

Polly Only thing is—you mustn't forget which tree you're nesting in. (*To*

Act I   13

Henry, invitingly) You keep close behind me, dear. (*She goes out through the archway*)
Henry Yes—rather! (*He is about to follow her*)
Sarah Henry!
Henry (*stopping, sheepishly*) Ah—er—bring the rest of the luggage, will you, Sarah?
Sarah (*obediently*) Yes, Henry.

She collects up the remaining things. Nora goes to assist

Nora Here—let me. I'll see to that.
Henry It's all right, Mrs Winthrop. She can manage.
Sarah Yes. I'm used to it by now.

She goes out, heavily laden, glaring at Henry as she goes

Henry looks suspiciously at Nora

Henry I hope you haven't made a lot of changes here since old Mrs Parker left.

Nora gives an ingenuous smile

Nora Oh, Chief Constable—as if I'd do anything like that! (*She starts to go*) Come on—I'll show you to your tree.

She goes out ahead of him. He follows in baleful silence

After a moment Roger comes in from the front door. He is a tall, thin man in a dark suit with a clerical collar. He looks the height of respectability. He looks about and, seeing nobody there, smiles broadly and optimistically. He closes the door quietly and moves down into the room, holding his hat. He spots one fishing-rod that Sarah has left behind, looks to left and right furtively, goes across, puts down his hat and picks up the rod with the secretive air of a naughty schoolboy. He essays a gentle cast

Nora returns through the archway and is well into the room before she sees a tall vicar casting an imaginary fly

Who the hell are you?

Roger freezes, the fishing-rod poised. He turns and sees her. She sees his clerical collar

Oh, God!

He smiles benignly

Roger No, but I'm from the same company.

He hastily puts the fishing-rod down. She crosses to him, anxiously

Nora What do *you* want?

Roger looks at his watch and taps it with a big, playful smile

Roger Nearly five o'clock.
Nora What about it?

Roger The bewitching hour. I telephoned and made a booking. Featherstone. Roger Featherstone. Don't you remember?

Nora goes and thumbs through a desk diary that is on the telephone table and sees Roger's name there. She puts the diary down, somewhat shamefaced

Nora Oh—yes—of course! Mr Featherstone. I clean forgot. I've had so many things on my mind, you see. Anyway, you're late! And you never said you were a vicar!
Roger I'm not.
Nora Then why are you dressed like that?
Roger You said on the telephone not to be too ostentatious. I thought this would lend an air of respectability to the proceedings.
Nora You can't come in here dressed like a vicar! You'll frighten my girls.
Roger Is anything the matter, Mrs Winthrop? You seem a little distraught.
Nora Oh, no! No—everything's fine! I was just going to look for the linen.
Roger I was told that the welcome here would be overwhelming...
Nora Yes. And normally it would be, but—you see—something unexpected has cropped up.
Roger Too many customers?
Nora N-no.
Roger Then what are we waiting for? (*With a big smile*) Lead on!
Nora I can't do that, Mr Featherstone. Not today. Not now.
Roger Don't tell me all your rooms are occupied?
Nora N-no. Not occupied. But we can't use them for the time being.
Roger Ah—plumbing? Something wrong with the pipes?
Nora N-no...

Roger has an appalling thought

Roger Not industrial dispute? Don't tell me your girls have gone on strike?
Nora N-no. Nothing like that. My girls are willing enough, but I can't let them work at the moment. (*Desperately*) Look, I can't explain now—but you've got to go! You can't stay here—not now! (*She crosses to* DR)
Roger But I've come all the way from Orpington.
Nora Well, you'll just have to go back there, dear. (*Urgently*) Look—certain people have arrived—and they could be dangerous, so—please, Mr Featherstone, don't ask questions—just go!

She goes quickly, DR

Roger stands, puzzled, confused and rather disappointed. He shrugs resignedly, picks up his hat, and is about to go when...

Henry comes in through the arch and sees him

Henry Ah! Good-afternoon, vicar.
Roger What? (*He puts his hand to his collar in panic*) Ah. Yes. Er—I—I was just going. (*He starts to go*)
Henry Don't be ridiculous. You've only just arrived.
Roger I think I've arrived at rather a bad time...!
Henry Never a bad time for the clergy to call. Jolly nice of you to pop in.

Act I 15

Roger Well, now I think I'll pop out again. (*He tries again*)
Henry Nonsense. You've probably travelled quite a distance to get here.
Roger Yes, I have . . .!
Henry Glass of sherry?
Roger I beg your pardon?
Henry Presumably you *are* allowed a glass of sherry from time to time?
Roger Well, I—I do have an occasional glass, yes.
Henry (*crossing to the drinks cupboard*) If you're anything like *our* vicar, you'll always be dipping into the communion wine. Sit down.
Roger What?
Henry Sit down. Save your legs. You want to keep your strength up, don't you?
Roger (*ruefully*) Not much point *now* . . . (*He puts his hat on the back of the sofa and sits down*)
Henry Must get awfully tired standing about in pulpits.
Roger Yes, I suppose so.
Henry What?
Roger (*quickly*) I mean—yes! It does. Very.

Henry pours the drinks

Henry Don't mind if I stick to whisky, do you? Don't want to change horses.
Roger No, no. You carry on.
Henry Right. I was hoping for cucumber sandwiches, but I suppose whisky'll have to do. (*He chuckles*)
Roger (*puzzled*) Cucumber sandwiches?
Henry Don't you like them?
Roger Oh—yes—rather!
Henry Well, there aren't any. Cheese and chutney any good?
Roger No, thanks.
Henry That's what *I* said. Pity they didn't know you were coming. They might have laid on something special for you.
Roger Yes, that's what I was hoping . . .!
Henry Still, I'm sure sherry will give you a lift.
Roger Who?
Henry (*arriving*) Sherry.
Roger Oh—thanks. (*He accepts the sherry*)

Jackie and Sally come running in through the archway

Jackie Have you seen Mrs Winthrop?
Henry I think she's searching for sheets.
Sally I wish I knew what was going on . . .
Jackie Do *you* know why she blew the whistle?
Henry No. I was wondering about that . . .
Jackie Did she fix you up all right?
Henry Oh, yes, thank you. I'm in Oak.
Jackie Oh, you'll like it in there.

Roger looks at the girls, hopefully

Roger Are either of you looking for me?

Jackie and Sally look at him in surprise and exchange a look

Jackie No. I don't think so.
Sally No. We've never had a vicar before.
Jackie You'll have to speak to Mrs Winthrop.

The girls giggle and run out through the archway

Henry Nice girls.
Roger Yes . . .
Henry Apparently Mrs Winthrop gets them from the Job Centre.
Roger (*astonished*) Really?!
Henry Well—cheers, vicar.
Roger Cheers.

They drink. Roger downs his in one. Henry looks at him, a little surprised

Henry Perhaps I should have brought the bottle.
Roger Oh, dear. I do seem to have drunk that rather quickly, don't I?
Henry Well, it was a bit brisk. Mind you, I don't drink with vicars very often so I've nothing to compare it with. Like another one?
Roger I wouldn't say no.
Henry I didn't think you would.

With an air of patient tolerance, Henry puts down his own glass and takes Roger's empty glass across to the drinks cupboard. He is about to refill the glass, thinks better of it, sets the sherry glass aside and pours a large amount of sherry into a tumbler. He brings it back to Roger

There you are. (*He puts the glass down on the table beside Roger*) That should keep you going for a few minutes.

Roger picks up the drink and looks at it, a trifle embarrassed

Roger Oh . . . er . . . thanks.
Henry (*picking up his own glass*) Well—cheers, vicar!
Roger Cheers . . .

Henry is about to drink, but stops to watch Roger, wondering if the large sherry will get the same treatment as the small one. Roger takes a very small delicate sip, his little finger raised, and smiles nervously at Henry

Have you . . . have you been here before?
Henry (*crossing above the sofa*) No. This is my first visit.
Roger Really?
Henry Oh, yes. I've heard a lot about it, of course.
Roger I'm sure you have! (*A little put out*) She found *you* a room, then?
Henry Sorry?
Roger She found *you* a room all right.
Henry Who?

Act I 17

Roger Mrs Winthrop!
Henry (*a little puzzled*) Well, of course she found me a room.
Roger Oh. Good.

A pause. Henry sits R *of Roger*

    Plumbing all right?
Henry Sorry?
Roger Taps in good working order?
Henry As far as I know.

A pause

    I'm in Oak.
Roger I beg your pardon?
Henry Oak.
Roger Ah. (*After a pause*) What are you talking about?
Henry Well, you see—all the rooms here are named after trees. I believe that was my brother's idea.
Roger Your brother?
Henry My brother Bernard. He named all the rooms after trees before he went off to the Orkneys.
Roger Ah! So it was through your brother that you knew about this place?
Henry Of course it was. Are you feeling all right, vicar?
Roger I'm not sure ...
Henry Bernard always enjoyed himself here.
Roger Is he enjoying himself in the Orkneys?
Henry Not very much. He's dead.
Roger Dead?
Henry Oh, yes. Fell off his tractor. I'm surprised they didn't arrange for you to do the service. The C of E always did excel at the graveside. Still, it's a long way to the Orkneys.

Roger finishes his sherry. Henry notices, begins to get up, but decides against it

Henry Oh, help yourself, vicar!
Roger Right. Thanks. (*He goes to get more sherry*)
Henry You must be trying for the Guinness Book of Records.

Debbie comes in DR. *She has changed into corduroy trousers, Wellington boots, a farmer's hat and a rather revealing shirt*

Debbie Look what she's made me put on. I ask you!
Henry Ah, that's better! Much more suitable for cleaning the cow-shed.
Debbie (*crossing to* C) *I* wouldn't know one end of a cow from the other ... (*She sees Roger and reacts*) Don't tell me *another* one's called on the off-chance!
Roger Certainly not! I was expected.
Debbie Oo, vicar—you are naughty! What would the bishop say?
Henry Debbie! That's no way to address the clergy.
Debbie Oh—sorry. (*To Roger*) Well, your reverence, if you've come here

for me, you're out of luck. (*Unable to believe it*) She's told me to sweep out the cow-shed.

She shrugs at Henry and goes out into the garden

Henry looks at Roger, puzzled

Henry Have you met her before?

Roger No. I've never *been* here before. (*He returns with his sherry replenished and resumes his seat*)

Henry So you must be new to the parish.

Roger (*with a smile*) Don't be silly . . .!

Henry is puzzled but decides not to pursue the matter. A pause. They raise their glasses and drink in silent and unconscious unison

Henry Sarah's in Ash.

Roger Sarah?

Henry Yes. She's my—er——

Roger Ah—yes—of course! (*Appalled at the thought*) You mean they've put her in a different room?

Henry I should jolly well hope so! Well, vicar, I very much appreciate your calling like this. But how did you know I was here?

Roger I didn't.

Henry Then why did you come here?

Roger Well—I've heard so much about the place. (*He leans towards Henry, confidentially*) I came all the way from Orpington.

Henry gazes at him in surprise

Henry But Orpington's miles away. The C of E must be awfully short of clergy. Must be a very big parish to spread all the way from Orpington to here.

Roger begins to giggle, the sherry taking effect. Henry looks at him

You feeling all right, vicar?

Which only makes Roger laugh even more!

Roger You don't think I'm *really* a vicar, do you?

Henry Sorry.

Roger leans on Henry's shoulder, confidentially

Roger I'm not a vicar.

Henry Not a vicar?

Roger I'm just *dressed* like a vicar.

Henry That's why I assumed that you *were* a vicar.

Roger Oh, no.

Henry I didn't know that.

Roger I'm just *pretending* to be a vicar.

Henry Really?

Roger Oh, yes. But I'm really here for the same thing as you are! (*He dives into his sherry again*)

Act I

Henry considers this in silence for a moment, then jumps to the wrong conclusion

Henry Ah! A spot of fishing?

Roger puts down his large glass of sherry

Roger What?
Henry (*smiling, delightedly*) You must be a friend of my brother's! I suppose he told you that you could come here and fish whenever you wanted to?

Nora returns with two pairs of sheets. She is appalled to see Roger still there — and talking to Henry!

Nora Oh, my God . . .!
Henry (*looking at her, sharply*) Mrs Winthrop!

Nora pretends to be pleased and moves above the sofa, smiling at Roger

Nora Ah! You're still here, then, vicar?
Henry (*intervening*) Mrs Winthrop——
Nora (*behind the sofa*) Yes?
Henry He's *not* a vicar.
Nora Of course he's a vicar! You're a vicar, aren't you, vicar?
Roger No! I told you, I'm here for——

Nora gives him a powerful push from behind which sends him sprawling on to the floor, where he inadvertently assumes an attitude of prayer. Nora turns to Henry with a smile and indicates the kneeling Roger

Nora See? He's a vicar.

Roger resumes his seat, ruffled. Nora moves to L of the sofa, clocking the large glass of sherry

I hope you haven't been giving the vicar sherry.
Henry Well, we did have a glass or two.
Nora Looks more like a bottle to me! (*T Roger, as if to a child*) Really, your reverence, you shouldn't be drinking sherry. Not when you're on duty. (*In her state of desperation, she unthinkingly finishes off the sherry and goes to put the empty glass down on the drinks cupboard and the sheets on the chair next to it*)

Henry and Roger watch her in astonishment and then exchange a look. Nora returns with a beaming smile

Very nice of his reverence to call, wasn't it, sir? He came up from the village specially to welcome you to the parish.
Henry No, he didn't. He came from Orpington.
Nora (*outraged*) Orpington? (*To Roger*) What you want to go and tell him a thing like that for? (*She gives him another push, sending him to his knees again*)
Roger But I *did* come from Orpington! I told you on the telephone that I was coming from Orpington!

Nora I don't know what's happening to the church these days. You don't seem to get the same class of clergy as you used to. Vicars aren't what they used to be.

Roger (*still on his knees*) I'm not a vicar! (*To Henry, plaintively*) I'm not a vicar.

Henry (*patting Roger's head*) There, there! That's all right. Nothing to worry about. *Every*one can't be a vicar.

Nora Don't you take any notice of him! He shouldn't have been drinking sherry.

Henry But, Mrs Winthrop, if this gentleman says he's not a vicar why shouldn't I believe him?

Nora And I suppose if the Archbishop of Canterbury came through that door and said he was a fishmonger, you'd believe that as well?

Henry (*puzzled*) Sorry?

Roger (*scrambling to his feet*) I think I'd better be going now ... (*He starts to go*)

Henry But you've only just arrived. You can't go all the way back to Orpington without even catching a fish.

Nora (*puzzled*) Fish? What fish?

Henry Trout! This gentleman is here to cast a fly.

Roger smiles, happily. Nora glares at him. He stops smiling. Nora turns to Henry again

Nora But if this gentleman isn't a vicar and has only come here for trout why should he dress up as a vicar?

Henry Ah—good question. We'd better ask him. (*He asks him*) Why did you come all the way from Orpington dressed as a vicar?

Roger, with the help of the sherry, begins to lose his patience

Roger Why the hell do you think? I told you. I came here for the same thing you did!

Nora is horrified at the revelation that seems to be imminent, and panics

Nora You'll have to forgive him, sir. He's under a bit of a strain. (*She grabs Roger's arm and drags him away from Henry to* DL) The Chief Constable is here on business!

Roger Chief Constable?

Nora Yes.

Roger On business?

Nora Yes! This house belongs to the Chief Constable's brother.

Roger The one who fell off his tractor?

Nora Yes! So the Chief Constable has come here to sort things out.

Roger (*fearfully*) Sort things out?

Nora Yes! With his sister.

Roger Sister?

Henry Sarah.

Roger Oh, dear God ...!

Nora That's more like it, vicar. We could do with a prayer.

Act I

Nora indicates Henry with a jerk or two of the head. Roger takes the hint and goes to Henry, assuming an attitude of ecclesiastical calm

Roger I don't think we've been properly introduced, have we?
Henry (*a little surprised*) Oh—all right. Please yourself. (*Extending his hand*) Henry Potterton. How do you do.
Roger (*as they shake hands*) Roger Featherstone. The *Reverend* Roger Featherstone.

Nora smiles, approvingly. Henry looks at Roger, bemused

I'm a vicar.
Henry I wish you'd make up your mind!
Nora Oh, he's just *so* full of fun! Always playing games. Aren't you, your reverence?
Roger (*crossing to Nora*) Well, yes, I do like a little joke, occasionally. (*He laughs, half-heartedly*)
Henry I hope you don't confuse your congregation like this. They might take the wrong path to the Pearly Gates.

Polly comes in through the archway wearing flat shoes, a plain but rather short dress, a white apron and a little hat, in the conventional style of a housemaid. She crosses to L of the sofa, curtsies, and smiles accommodatingly at Henry

Polly There you are, sir. Is that better for you?
Henry Ah—yes. That's more like it.
Polly (*to Roger*) He prefers me dressed like this. Bit kinky, if you ask me. But there's no accounting for taste. (*She reacts*) Oh, my God! It's a vicar!
Nora Polly, that is no way to address the clergy!
Roger (*benignly*) I—I just popped in to ... to see how you're all getting along. You know—keep an eye on my flock.
Polly (*to Nora*) The tone of this place hasn't half gone up. First of all we get a Chief Constable. Now we've got a vicar. We'll be having the Prince of Wales next!
Roger (*anxious to be on his way*) Well, I think I'll be on my way. (*He goes to collect his hat from the back of the sofa*)
Nora (*sharply*) Where are *you* off to?

Roger stops in his tracks, nervously

Roger I do have other calls to make.
Henry Well, if you drink the same amount of sherry everywhere you go, you'll never make it back to the vestry.
Nora (*smiling, sweetly*) I think you'd better stay here for the time being, your reverence.
Roger Do you?
Nora (*severely*) Yes, I do!
Roger Oh, very well ... (*Reluctantly, he drifts towards the window-seat*)

Sarah comes in from the garden and crosses to Nora

Sarah I've just seen a man disappearing down the drive on a bicycle.
Polly (*to Nora*) That'll be the bank manager.
Roger (*grinning, knowingly, at Henry*) Another satisfied customer!
Henry What are you talking about?

Roger is puzzled by Henry's attitude, shrugs and looks out of the window at the cows

Sarah He seemed in a dreadful hurry to get away.
Polly I'm not surprised . . .!
Sarah Pedalling like mad. Rather reckless, I thought.
Henry A bank manager on a bicycle? Didn't he have his car with him?
Polly Don't be daft! He wouldn't want people to see his car parked outside *here*, would he? (*She giggles*)
Nora (*glaring at her*) Polly!
Henry So he came here on a bicycle?
Polly Oh, no. The bicycle belongs to the window-cleaner.
Sarah I didn't know there was a window-cleaner . . .
Nora Oh, yes. He always comes on Wednesday.

Sarah is quite moved by the generosity of the window-cleaner

Sarah Aaah . . . how kind of him to lend his bicycle to the bank manager.
Polly He didn't lend it to him—he *took* it! I saw him from the window. He just grabbed it and made off!
Sarah Didn't the window-cleaner try to stop him?
Polly Yes, he did—but he fell off his ladder! (*She laughs*)
Sarah Poor man. Is he all right?
Polly How do I know? I was changing my clothes, wasn't I?

Debbie comes in from the garden

Debbie Mrs Winthrop! How on earth am I supposed to clean the cow-shed?
Nora (*crossing to Debbie, grimly*) How do you *usually* clean the cow-shed?
Debbie I don't!
Nora With a broom, Debbie! With a broom!

Debbie sees Polly in a maid's outfit and laughs

Debbie Here—what's she dressed up like that for?
Nora She's serving tea.
Debbie Well, that makes a change!

She laughs again, and Polly gives her a look

Sarah (*thoughtfully*) I do hope the window-cleaner's all right . . .

Roger makes another attempt to escape

Roger I really think I must be going——

Sarah notices him for the first time and exclaims, delightedly

Sarah Good heavens! Henry, have you noticed?

Act I 23

Henry What?
Sarah There's a vicar over there.
Henry If he *is* a vicar. Doesn't seem able to make up his mind.

Sarah advances on Roger, the gracious hostess

Sarah Vicar—how nice of you to call.
Roger Well, I—I was just passing, so I thought I'd look in.
Sarah (*to Roger, appalled*) Has nobody offered you tea?
Henry He's teetotal.
Sarah What?
Henry Totally off tea and totally on sherry.
Sarah Polly! Cucumber sandwiches for the vicar.
Polly (*cross*) There aren't any cucumbers!
Sarah Oh, what a pity. We always have cucumber sandwiches when the clergy call. (*She smiles at Roger*)
Polly You can have cheese and chutney if you like.
Roger No—really. Thank you all the same.
Nora Well, it's all you're going to get *here* today!
Roger Yes, I know ...!
Sarah (*to Roger*) It's going to be a beautiful evening. Would you like to have a look at the garden?
Roger Well, I ...
Henry The vicar doesn't want to go trundling around the garden.
Sarah Why not? After all, we do have a lot to talk to him about.
Roger (*nervously*) Do you?
Nora Do you?
Henry Do we?
Sarah Henry and I had a brother who went into your line of business.
Debbie (*to Polly*) What are they on about?
Polly I dunno.
Sarah We can talk about it while we're walking around the garden.
Nora But it's very wet underfoot. You'll spoil your shoes.
Sarah We can put our boots on. They're outside in the car. Come along, Henry. The fresh air will do us good.

Henry and Sarah start for the front door

Roger But I haven't got any boots.
Sarah I'm sure we'll find you a spare pair.
Henry What size do you take?
Roger Ten.
Henry Splendid! You can borrow *hers*. (*Indicating Nora*)

Henry and Sarah go out to the front door to find their boots

Debbie I wish I knew what was going on ...

Jackie and Sally come in through the archway

Jackie Has something happened, Mrs Winthrop?
Nora It soon will if you don't get some proper clothes on!

Polly (*to Sally*) Did you get rid of your chap?
Sally Yes, but he wasn't very pleased. He hadn't even got his tie off.
Polly I knew the customers wouldn't like it, Mrs Winthrop.
Nora Well, I hadn't any choice, had I?
Jackie I wish I knew what this is all about . . .
Nora It's about the Chief Constable, Jackie! That's what it's all about.
Roger (*moving to below the sofa*) Why didn't you tell me straight away that he wasn't here for "you-know-what"?
Nora I didn't get the chance, did I?
Roger I thought he was one of us! (*He sinks in despair on to the sofa*)
Sally Isn't he?
Nora Of course he isn't!
Debbie Oh, my gawd . . .
Polly You mean he isn't here for "you-know-what"?
Nora He doesn't even know that "you-know-what"'s been going on!
Debbie Oh, my gawd . . .
Jackie Then what *is* he here for?
Nora He's here because this house belongs to his brother.
Polly So what will he do if he finds out what's been going on here?
Nora What do you think? He's a policeman. He'll shoot first and ask questions afterwards.
Debbie Oh, my gawd . . .
Sally And didn't his brother know about "you-know-what", either?
Nora Of course he didn't! There was none of that going on before he went off to the Orkneys!
Roger You mean *you* started it all after he'd gone?
Nora Of course I did, dear. (*Reasonably*) Well, it's such a very big house. And I'm a warm-hearted woman. I didn't see the harm in it, vicar.
Roger I'm not a vicar!
Nora Yes, you are!
Roger What?
Nora They think you're a vicar, so you're going to *be* a bloody vicar. You'll lend a little respectability to the place.
Roger But my wife will be wanting me home for dinner.
Nora If you don't co-operate your wife won't be wanting you home at all.
Roger You wouldn't tell her?!
Nora Yes, I would!
Jackie What are we going to do, then?
Nora We're going to act respectable! Behave like you would if you worked here properly. Make the tea, peel the potatoes, feed the pigs, all that sort of thing.
Roger I really must be going . . .!
Nora You're staying here! Polly, you go and make sure the rest of the rooms are empty. We don't want any *more* customers making a dash for it. And take those sheets with you. Debbie, you go back to the cow-shed. Jackie and Sally—change your clothes and go and see to the chickens!

The girls start to go

Act I 25

And girls!

They hesitate

If you see any *more* men arriving—send 'em away!

The girls all run out in different directions. Polly picks up the sheets and goes out through the archway, Debbie into the garden, Jackie and Sally DR

(*To Roger*) And you go outside and have a walk in the garden like she said.
Roger But I'd rather go——
Nora In the garden!
Roger Oh, very well ... (*He starts to go*)
Nora And don't forget that you're a bloody vicar!

Roger goes out into the garden, gloomily

The telephone rings. Nora answers it

Hullo? ... Yes, speaking. ... What? (*She reacts in alarm*) No! None of my girls are available! ... Because it's the Spring Bank Holiday, that's why not! (*She hangs up*) Oh, my God ...! (*Her eyes settle on the drinks cupboard. She goes to it, quickly, glances around and then pours out the last of the sherry. She downs it in one*)

Mr Tunnicliffe comes in, tentatively, from the front door. He is a small man of about sixty. He wears a dark suit and a hat, and carries a black briefcase. He looks about, obviously a stranger. He sees Nora's back

Mr Tunnicliffe Ah!

Nora turns and sees him. She looks aghast. He smiles, rather nervously

The door was open so I came straight in.
Nora Oh, no! Not *another* one?
Mr Tunnicliffe (*surprised*) I beg your pardon?
Nora (*advancing on him*) I suppose *you*'ve come here looking for a girl, as well?
Mr Tunnicliffe A girl?
Nora If you're expecting what I think you're expecting you'd better go elsewhere because you won't get it here.
Mr Tunnicliffe (*non-plussed*) This *is* Dingle Farm, isn't it?
Nora Now, look here—whatever you've heard, it isn't true. This is a respectable house. So you be on your way!
Mr Tunnicliffe Oh, dear. I hope I haven't been given the wrong address. I've never been here before, you see.
Nora And you can't stay here now!
Mr Tunnicliffe (*crossing to the sofa*) But if this is Dingle Farm, I bring you glad tidings of great joy.
Nora If you're hoping for a Christmas box, you're about seven months too soon. Go on—hop it!

Mr Tunnicliffe But I have business here. (*He sits on the sofa with his briefcase*)
Nora (*going to him*) Not any more you haven't! The situation has changed, so whatever you had in your mind put it out of your mind, because it's not going to happen. Not today. And nobody invited you to sit down!
Mr Tunnicliffe But it's such a long way up from the village.
Nora Don't tell me you *walked* up from the village?
Mr Tunnicliffe Oh, no. No. Dear me, no. I came on horseback.
Nora (*rather taken aback*) Horseback?
Mr Tunnicliffe Well, I tried to get a taxi at the station, but there were none about.
Nora So you got a horse instead?
Mr Tunnicliffe Yes. I spotted this riding school, you see. They hire them out by the hour. They were a little taken aback at first by my request.
Nora I'm not surprised. I mean, you're not exactly dressed like the Lone Ranger, are you, dear?
Mr Tunnicliffe Ah—but I am no stranger to the saddle. I used to be a jockey. In my younger days.
Nora You must have caused quite a stir riding through the streets dressed like that.
Mr Tunnicliffe One or two heads did turn, I must confess.
Nora And where have you left Black Beauty, then?
Mr Tunnicliffe I tethered him to the fence.
Nora Well, you'd better untether him and ride off into the sunset because you can't hang around here. (*She tries to pull him to his feet*)
Mr Tunnicliffe But I've only just arrived.
Nora Look, I'm in enough trouble already, and if anyone finds *you* here there'll be hell to pay.

Polly comes racing in through the archway

Polly Mrs Winthrop! There's a horse at the door!
Nora Yes. It's his.

Polly looks at Mr Tunnicliffe in surprise. He waves a greeting, smiling happily

Polly We've never had a client arrive on horseback before. (*To Nora*) He's not expected, is he?
Nora Of course he's not expected!
Mr Tunnicliffe I called on the off-chance. But it is rather urgent.
Nora That's what they all say. You can't stay here!

Debbie runs in from the garden

Debbie Mrs Winthrop! There's a horse at the door!
Nora }
Polly } (*together*) It's *his*!
Debbie We've never had a client arrive on horseback before. He's not expected, is he?
Nora }
Polly } (*together*) Of course he's not expected!

Act I   27

Mr Tunnicliffe I came on business.
Nora That's what they all say.
Debbie You can't stay here!
Nora He knows that.
Debbie What if the Chief Constable finds him?
Mr Tunnicliffe (*cheering up*) Chief Constable?
Nora (*to Polly*) Where is he now?
Polly He was by the summer-house a moment ago. I'll have a look. (*She goes to the window*)
Mr Tunnicliffe Do I understand that the Chief Constable is in the summer-house?
Polly Not any more. He's coming this way!
Debbie Oh, my gawd ...!
Nora (*to Mr Tunnicliffe*) You see, the Chief Constable doesn't know about "you-know-what".
Mr Tunnicliffe (*puzzled*) You-know-what?
Nora Exactly! And if he finds out there'll be hell to pay.
Polly He's coming!
Nora Polly—Debbie—go and distract him!
Polly What?
Debbie How?
Nora You should know! Delay him while I get rid of the jockey.

Polly and Debbie race out into the garden

Nora turns, urgently, to Mr Tunnicliffe

Come along! Up you get!
Mr Tunnicliffe Where are we going?
Nora You're going in here.

She leads the astonished Mr Tunnicliffe across to a big cupboard DL

Come on! It'll only be for a few minutes, dear. I'll get him out of the way, and as soon as it's all clear I'll let you know.

She opens the cupboard door, which creaks. Mr Tunnicliffe naturally looks rather surprised

Mr Tunnicliffe But that's a cupboard.
Nora Yes. I know.
Mr Tunnicliffe Couldn't I wait elsewhere?
Nora You might be seen elsewhere. In you go, dear.
Mr Tunnicliffe I didn't come here on horseback just to stand in a cupboard.
Nora Oh—all right. (*She goes and picks up a stool and puts it inside the cupboard*) There you are. Now you can sit down.

Mr Tunnicliffe is totally bewildered

It'll only be for a few minutes.

She pushes him gently but firmly into the cupboard. But his head pops out again

Mr Tunnicliffe I always get very thirsty when I'm sitting in a cupboard.

Nora grabs the bottle of whisky and hands it to him. He is looking a little more pleased as she shuts the door on him

Aaaah . . .

Henry comes in from the front door, looking back outside as he does so. He is now wearing Wellington boots. He moves into the room, thoughtfully, and looks at Nora

She is standing nervously, guarding the cupboard door

Henry Mrs Winthrop! There's a horse at the front door!

Nora has temporarily forgotten about the horse, so she rather over-reacts to the news

Nora What's it doing out there?
Henry Nothing very much. Just standing there. Chewing the grass a little. You know what they're like. (*He looks in the direction of the horse*)

The cupboard door creaks open. Nora hastily slams it shut again. Henry turns at the sound

What was that?
Nora *I* didn't hear anything.
Henry Extraordinary . . . Have you any idea who that horse belongs to?
Nora No!
Henry It wasn't there when we arrived.
Nora Are you sure?
Henry I think I'd have noticed.
Nora Oh, it . . . it probably wandered in off the common.
Henry Are there horses on the common?
Nora Oh, yes! Dozens of them. Wild horses. All over the common.
Henry I don't think this is a wild horse.
Nora It could be.
Henry I doubt it. It's wearing a bridle and saddle. (*He looks towards the horse again*)

The cupboard door creaks open. Nora hastily slams it shut. Henry turns at the sound

There it was again.
Nora What?
Henry You must have heard it that time.
Nora No. I didn't hear anything.

Henry pulls his ear a little

Henry I shall have to have a check-up.
Nora (*suddenly*) Ah! I know where it came from!
Henry The noise?

Act I

Nora The horse. It'll be from the riding school in the village. Of course! Why didn't I think of that before? Those horses are a bit frisky, and sometimes they lose their riders and run around loose for hours. I expect that's what happened to this one — lost its rider and ran in here.
Henry If it did, it's tied itself up to the fence.

Nora makes a desperate attempt to get rid of Henry. She goes to him urgently

Nora You needn't worry about the horse! You leave the horse to me, Chief Constable. You carry on with your walk and I'll see to the horse.

She grabs his arm and tries to urge him towards the garden, but he eludes her and heads for the sofa in his boots

Henry No, no. I think I've had enough walking for the time being. I'll just sit down here for a while.
Nora No, you can't!
Henry Why not?
Nora Your sister's out there with the vicar. You can't leave your sister alone with a vicar.
Henry Oh, Sarah's quite used to handling the clergy.

He starts to sit down, but she stops him

Nora You can't sit there!
Henry Why not?
Nora You've got boots on! You'll put mud all over the carpet. Your brother wouldn't like to think you were sitting in here with your boots on.
Henry You've never met my brother.
Nora No, of course I haven't!
Henry Well, there you are, then. For all you know, he may have sat about all day with his boots on. So perhaps you'd be good enough to pour me a whisky.
Nora What?
Henry A large whisky and a little water.
Nora There isn't any.
Henry No water?
Nora No whisky.
Henry I had some earlier on.
Nora You can't drink whisky with your boots on!
Henry Very well — if it'll make you happy — I'll take them off. (*He lifts one foot off the ground*)
Nora In *here*?
Henry Certainly. Come on — give me a hand!

Reluctantly, Nora helps him pull off one boot. He then lifts the other foot and she tries that, but it is more difficult than the other. She pulls hard. The boot comes off suddenly and she goes shooting backwards with the momentum, holding the boot. At that moment, the cupboard door opens again. Nora staggers back and hits the cupboard door, closing it with a bang yet again. Henry reacts to the sound

There! You must have heard it that time!
Nora I was running backwards. I can't hear anything when I'm running backwards.

Henry raises his stocking feet, happily

Henry There! That better?
Nora (*crossing to him, appalled*) A Chief Constable sitting in the sitting-room in his socks?
Henry (*irritably*) Oh, very well! I'll go and get some shoes. But while I'm away, you pour me a whisky. I shall expect to find a large glass waiting here when I return. There! On that table.
Nora I'll do my best . . .
Henry Right!

He stomps out through the archway in his socks

Nora goes quickly to the cupboard and opens the door. Mr Tunnicliffe looks out

Mr Tunnicliffe Is it all clear now?

He walks out of the cupboard, but Nora catches his arm and restrains him

Nora No, it isn't! Get back inside! (*She pushes him back into the cupboard*) And give that to me. (*She grabs the bottle from him*)
Mr Tunnicliffe But I haven't had my drink yet.
Nora Well, whose fault is that, dear? Stay in there until I tell you. (*She closes the door on the protesting Mr Tunnicliffe and goes quickly to the drinks. She pours a large measure of whisky, puts the bottle down, adds the smallest drop of water and crosses with the whisky to put it down on the table beside the sofa as instructed*)

Polly and Debbie come running in from the garden

Polly Here—Mrs Winthrop! You know that horse that was tied up outside?
Nora I'm far too busy to think about horses at the moment, Polly——
Polly But it's got away!
Nora The horse?
Debbie Yes! And now it's wandering about in the vegetable garden!
Nora Oh, no!
Debbie He'll be trampling all the cabbages to bits!
Nora Well, go and stop him, then!
Debbie Stop him?
Nora Oh, come on! (*She heads for the garden*)
Polly How are we going to stop him?
Nora Don't ask me! I'm not used to handling horses . . .

They go out into the garden

The moment they have gone, a hooded figure comes in from the front door, wearing a brown cassock and sandals. He sighs, contentedly, and puts back

Act I

the hood. *We now see that it is Henry's twin brother, Bernard. (And, of course, played by the same actor). He looks about*

Bernard Mrs Parker!

He goes towards the archway, but stops as the cupboard door creaks slowly open. He takes cover by the french windows and watches in astonishment as a small man in a dark suit comes out of the cupboard cautiously, tiptoes to the drinks, picks up the bottle of whisky and tiptoes back again with a satisfied smile. Bernard stares in disbelief. Mr Tunnicliffe disappears back into the cupboard with the whisky and closes the door behind him, without noticing the hidden Bernard. Bernard drifts to the sofa in a daze and sits down. He looks towards the cupboard, bewildered

Jackie and Sally come running in, DR, *still scantily clad. They see the strange figure in a cassock. They scream and run away above the sofa and out through the archway*

Bernard sees them disappearing, and looks surprised. He also sees the large glass of whisky. He picks it up and drinks it down in one

Black-out

The CURTAIN *falls*

ACT II

Scene 1

The same. A few minutes later

Bernard has now gone, leaving the empty whisky glass on the table beside the sofa

Henry comes in through the archway. He has now got his shoes on. He crosses to the sofa and picks up the glass of whisky he is expecting to find. He sees that it is empty and looks puzzled. He sighs heavily, puts the glass down again and goes to the drinks cupboard. He cannot find the whisky. He searches, unable to understand where it has gone

The cupboard door creaks open, slowly, hiding Henry behind it and Mr Tunnicliffe peers out. He cannot see Henry behind the door and tiptoes up to the drinks cupboard, still carrying the bottle of whisky. He finds a suitable glass, picks it up and tiptoes back to his cupboard. He goes inside and closes the door after him, revealing the astonished Henry behind it. Henry considers for a moment, then knocks on the cupboard door. The door opens slowly and Mr Tunnicliffe looks out. He sees Henry and smiles, as if it was quite usual to appear out of a cupboard carrying a bottle of whisky

Mr Tunnicliffe Oh—were you looking for the whisky?

Henry glares at him, balefully, and grabs the bottle from him

Henry Yes, I was, as a matter of fact. Do you *always* hide in a cupboard with a bottle of whisky?
Mr Tunnicliffe No. This is my first time. It was quite a new experience.
Henry Well, I hope it's not going to become a habit. I don't like people popping out of cupboards. (*He wanders away with the bottle*)

Mr Tunnicliffe closes the cupboard door

Mr Tunnicliffe She told me to wait in there until the coast was clear.

Henry stops and looks at him

Henry Who did?
Mr Tunnicliffe The lady who put me in the cupboard.
Henry A lady put you in the cupboard?
Mr Tunnicliffe Yes. Popped me in and closed the door.
Henry With the whisky.
Mr Tunnicliffe Yes.

Act II, Scene 1   33

Henry Lucky for you. (*He goes to pour some whisky into his glass*) Who are you, anyway?
Mr Tunnicliffe My name is Tunnicliffe. I'm a solicitor.

Henry turns, his eyes lighting up, hopefully

Henry Of Tunnicliffe, Tunnicliffe, Tipthorpe and Tunnicliffe?
Mr Tunnicliffe The very same. Have you seen the Chief Constable?
Henry I *am* the Chief Constable.
Mr Tunnicliffe (*moving in a little*) Ah! Then I have news!
Henry News?
Mr Tunnicliffe About your brother.
Henry (*crossing to him*) My brother Bernard?
Mr Tunnicliffe Yes. I bring you glad tidings of great joy! (*He smiles, happily*)
Henry I wouldn't have thought falling off a tractor and killing yourself was anything to rejoice about.
Mr Tunnicliffe Ah—well, that's the point.
Henry What?
Mr Tunnicliffe He did, but he isn't.
Henry Did but isn't?
Mr Tunnicliffe He did fall off his tractor, but he isn't dead.
Henry Not dead?
Mr Tunnicliffe Alive and well!
Henry My brother?
Mr Tunnicliffe Yes.
Henry But you told us he was dead! How the hell could you make a mistake like that?
Mr Tunnicliffe Ah—well, you see—Mr Tipthorpe looks after the northern area, and I'm afraid he's a little ... er ...
Henry Vague?
Mr Tunnicliffe Oh, yes.
Henry Gaga?
Mr Tunnicliffe I'm afraid so. Mind you—a natural mistake. Apparently it was the other one.
Henry What other one?
Mr Tunnicliffe The other Mr Potterton.
Henry You mean there are two Pottertons up there?
Mr Tunnicliffe Yes. One alive and one dead.
Henry Well, I'm glad you told me before we set off for the funeral. It's a long drive to the Orkneys. Oh, that is splendid! Not dead, after all. Sarah *will* be pleased.
Mr Tunnicliffe I'm sure.
Henry Oh, yes. She's a very poor traveller. Alive and well, eh?
Mr Tunnicliffe And coming here!
Henry Alive and well and coming here?
Mr Tunnicliffe On his way. Arriving soon.

Nora comes in from the front door, a trifle breathless

(*Seeing her*) Ah—here she is! This is the lady who put me in the cupboard.

Nora sees Mr Tunnicliffe and goes to him, urgently

Nora Come on, you—out!

She grabs his arm and tries to pull him away. Mr Tunnicliffe resists. Henry, between them, looks on, astonished

Mr Tunnicliffe Let go of my arm!
Nora I told you not to hang about. Come on! Let's be having you! (*She pulls him across to her and pushes him towards the front door*)
Henry Just a minute, Mrs Winthrop!

They stop

Nora Don't you worry, sir. I'll get rid of him. Come on, you! (*She tries again*)
Henry Mrs Winthrop!

They stop again

This gentleman was in a cupboard.
Nora In a cupboard?
Henry And he says *you* put him there.

Nora snorts, disdainfully

Nora Well, they all say that, don't they? I've met his sort before and they all say that.
Mr Tunnicliffe She put me in the cupboard!
Nora You see? What did I tell you?

Henry is trying to make sense out of what he is hearing

Mr Tunnicliffe She put me in the cupboard! *And* gave me a bottle of whisky!
Nora (*laughing*) That's likely, isn't it?
Henry Well, he did have a bottle with him when he came out of the cupboard.
Nora He must have pinched it, then, mustn't he? Don't you worry, sir. I'll get rid of him. (*To Mr Tunnicliffe*) Now, come on, dear. There's a good boy. We've caught your horse for you, so you get back on to the saddle and trot off home.
Henry Don't tell me that horse outside belongs to you?
Mr Tunnicliffe I hired it in the village.
Henry You came here on horseback?
Mr Tunnicliffe Yes.
Henry Dressed like that?

Debbie comes running in from the garden

Debbie Mrs Winthrop! We've lost him again!
Nora Who?

Act II, Scene 1   35

Debbie The horse! He got away!
Nora Oh, Debbie! For heaven's sake! I told you to hang on to him and tie him up.
Debbie We tried, but we couldn't! Polly's chasing after him across the field!
Mr Tunnicliffe (*appalled*) Oh, no! Now I shall forfeit my deposit! (*He runs towards the garden*)
Nora You go with him, Debbie. Show him which way they went.

Mr Tunnicliffe disappears into the garden with Debbie following behind him

Henry (*handing her his empty glass*) I'd better go and find Sarah. She *will* be pleased. (*He makes for the archway*)
Nora About the horse?
Henry About the good news. It isn't every day that someone comes back from the dead.

He grins and goes off through the archway

Nora looks puzzled, shrugs it off, collects the bottle of whisky and takes it and the empty glass back to the drinks table

Roger comes in from the front door in a high state of alarm

Roger Mrs Winthrop!
Nora (*jumping*) Aah! (*She sees him and relaxes*) Oh, Mr Featherstone—you made me jump.
Roger There's a man in Sycamore!
Nora (*crossing to him*) Now, don't be silly, dear. The bank manager was in Sycamore and *he* went off on a bicycle.
Roger Well, there's someone in there now! I caught a glimpse of him through the window. Fast asleep!
Nora Oh, all right. I'll have a look. You go and keep the Chief Constable out of the way.
Roger I can't do that!
Nora Why not?
Roger I can't! I won't!
Nora (*sweetly*) Oh, Mr Featherstone—what would your wife think if she knew you weren't being helpful?
Roger I can . . .! I will . . .!
Nora And while you're doing that, I'll go and see who it is who's having a kip in Sycamore.

They go, quickly; he through the arch, she through the front door

Bernard comes in DR, *eating a piece of bread and cheese. He is about to sit on the sofa, but hesitates and looks towards the cupboard, remembering. He goes across, opens the door carefully and peers inside. Nobody there. He shrugs, thinking he must have been seeing things previously, and goes back to the sofa to sit down with his bread and cheese*

Polly comes racing in from the garden, breathlessly. She sees a figure in a cassock and screams

Bernard turns. Polly relaxes, thinking it is Henry, and goes to him

Polly Oh, it's you, sir! You did give me a fright. What you dressed up like that for?
Bernard These days I always dress like this.
Polly (*puzzled*) What? For dinner?
Bernard (*amused*) Dinner, breakfast—anytime!
Polly You mean... whenever the mood takes you... you go and slip into that thing?
Bernard I've been doing it for quite a few months now.
Polly (*giggling*) Have you really? Oo, you are kinky! (*She pushes him, playfully*)

Bernard is rather taken aback

Bernard What?
Polly Well—first I have to go and dress up like *this*, then you go and dress up like *that*!
Bernard (*puzzled*) Were you one of the girls who came through here just now?
Polly No. I've been chasing the horse.
Bernard (*totally bemused*) Chasing a horse?
Polly It was crushing the cabbages. Poor Debbie's still running about trying to catch it.
Bernard Well, perhaps I'd better introduce myself——
Polly (*laughing*) You don't have to do that!
Bernard But if we've never met before——
Polly Course we've met before! You didn't like me walking about with so little on. Not when you were after cucumber sandwiches.
Bernard Sorry?
Polly That's why I changed into this.
Bernard Oh, you mustn't dress up like that...
Polly You *asked* me to!
Bernard I did?
Polly Yes! You remember—flat shoes, plain dress, white apron, little hat.
Bernard But I don't approve of class distinctions. You do an honest job of work, don't you?
Polly (*smiling, modestly*) Well, I think I give satisfaction, yes...
Bernard Don't let me see you demeaning yourself by dressing up like that again. We're all equal. Just you remember that.
Polly (*confused*) All equal. Yes, sir. Thank you, sir.
Bernard So off you go and change.
Polly Now?
Bernard Now. And don't ever let me see you dressed in a uniform again.

Polly cannot understand the apparent about-face of "Henry"

Polly But I thought you——
Bernard (*with a gentle smile*) No argument now. All equal. Go and change.

Act II, Scene 1   37

Polly All equal. Go and change. Right you are, sir. Right away, sir. (*She pauses on her way out, and turns back to him*) All equal?
Bernard (*joyfully*) That's more like it! *Now* you're getting the idea.
Polly Yes, sir. Thank you, sir. All equal . . .

Polly staggers off DR, *in a cloud of bewilderment*

Bernard watches her go, with the beneficient smile of a man who is putting the world to rights

Roger comes rushing in through the archway

Roger I can't find him anywhere! He must have gone back into the garden——! (*He stops when he sees Bernard—or, as he thinks, Henry in a cassock*) Oh, my God . . .!

Bernard smiles at the new arrival, rises and goes to him

Bernard Ah! Good-afternoon, vicar. Well—this *is* a surprise! (*He shakes Roger's hand*)
Roger Yes—it certainly is! (*He gazes in astonishment at "Henry's" mode of dress*)
Bernard I take it you're new to the parish?

Roger stares at him, glassily

Roger What?
Bernard Well, we've never met *before*, have we?
Roger What are you talking about?
Bernard My sister will be very pleased you called. She is a firm devotee of the C of E. I'll go and find her.
Roger No! I'll go!
Bernard (*with a smile*) I doubt very much if you'd know where to look. Leave it to me. I know my way about. (*He starts to go*)
Roger Has your sister seen you dressed up like that before?
Bernard No. I don't believe she has. It'll be quite a surprise for her!

He goes through the archway

Roger looks after him, puzzled

Nora comes in from the front door in a state of alarm

Nora Mr Featherstone!
Roger (*jumping*) Aaah!
Nora (*going to him, urgently*) You were right about Sycamore! There *is* a man lying down in there!
Roger Oh, God . . .!
Nora No, dear. The window-cleaner.
Roger The one who fell off his ladder?
Nora Yes!
Roger What's he doing lying down in Sycamore?
Nora *I* don't know, dear. I expect he staggered in there after his fall.
Roger Did you get rid of him?

Nora No. I couldn't.
Roger Why not?
Nora He's dead!
Roger Dead?!
Nora Well, he's very still. And *I* couldn't wake him. He probably hit his head when he fell off his ladder.

Roger starts to go towards the front door

Where are *you* going?
Roger I'm not staying in a house with a dead window-cleaner.
Nora Oh, yes, you are! We've got to get him out of there.
Roger Oh, no! (*He starts to go*)
Nora Oh, yes! (*She restrains him*)
Roger Couldn't we just ring the police?
Nora The police are already here!
Roger What?
Nora The Chief Constable! That's why you're going to help me get the window-cleaner out of Sycamore.
Roger Where shall we put him?
Nora *I* don't know! But we can't leave him there.

Jackie and Sally come running in from the garden

Jackie Mrs Winthrop! We've been looking for you!
Nora What is it, dear?
Jackie We saw a monk on the sofa!
Nora A monk?
Sally Well, he was dressed like a monk.
Roger (*impatiently*) That was the Chief Constable!
Jackie What was he dressed up like that for?
Roger *I* don't know!
Nora We've got bigger problems than that at the moment, Jackie. Go and change your clothes!

Jackie and Sally shrug, helplessly, at each other and run out again DR

Come on, then, Mr Featherstone! Let's go and see about the window-cleaner.

They are about to go towards the front door, but ...

Mr Tunnicliffe staggers in from the garden, half-supported by Debbie. He is breathless

Mr Tunnicliffe I can't think how I ever took up riding in the first place.
Debbie Poor thing. He's quite exhausted.
Nora I thought I told you to go home!
Debbie Oh, don't shout at him, Mrs Winthrop. He can hardly stand up. (*To Mr Tunnicliffe*) Come on, dear ...
Mr Tunnicliffe It's all right. I can manage. (*He heads for the sofa, sees Roger*

Act II, Scene 1

for the first time and tries to rally a little) Ah, vicar! How nice of you to call! (*He continues to the sofa and sits down*)
Roger (*to Nora*) Who the hell is this?
Nora It doesn't matter! It's of no importance! Did you catch the horse, Debbie?
Debbie Yes, but it was a hell of a chase.
Mr Tunnicliffe (*to Roger*) I presume you're here to bless this house?
Roger Well, no—not exactly. I'm here for a bit of——
Nora Rubbish!
Mr Tunnicliffe What?
Nora He's here to get rid of the rubbish. Off you go, vicar! You know where it is. (*She pushes Roger towards the archway*)
Roger (*nervously*) Where what is?
Nora The rubbish you came to collect!
Roger No—I won't!
Nora Yes—you *will*!

She pushes Roger rather more forcefully than she intended ...

And he goes flying out through the archway, rather spectacularly

You'd better go and keep an eye on the horse, Debbie dear. We don't want him getting loose again.

Debbie runs out into the garden

Now, look here—there isn't much time.
Mr Tunnicliffe (*apprehensively*) Oh, dear. You're not going to put me back in the cupboard, are you?
Nora Not if you do what I tell you. You see, the Chief Constable doesn't know what's been going on here.

Mr Tunnicliffe is not very clear either

Mr Tunnicliffe I'm not surprised! Neither do I.
Nora So whatever happens don't tell him who you are.
Mr Tunnicliffe He already knows.
Nora (*as if to a child*) Then you'll have to pretend to be somebody else, dear.
Mr Tunnicliffe (*bemused*) Why?
Nora If the Chief Constable finds out what you're here for, he'll probably shoot you!
Mr Tunnicliffe But I told him what I'm here for.
Nora Well, now you can tell him it was a mistake! Take my word for it. If you want to go living—pretend to be somebody else!

She goes, quickly, through the archway

Mr Tunnicliffe is left in a cloud of bewilderment and thinks at once of alcohol. He hastens to the drinks cupboard. He has the whisky bottle in his hand and is about to pour a glass when ...

Henry comes in from the garden

Henry Good God! Are you drinking *again*?

Mr Tunnicliffe reacts in alarm and freezes, fearing firearms, his back to Henry, his arms raised

Mr Tunnicliffe Don't shoot, sir! I can explain!
Henry Shoot? How can I shoot without a gun?
Mr Tunnicliffe You mean you're not . . . armed, sir?
Henry Of course I'm not armed.
Mr Tunnicliffe (*relieved*) Thank God for that . . .! (*He turns to face Henry, the bottle in his hand*)
Henry Ah! I see you've found the whisky. (*He chuckles, playfully*) Not going back in the cupboard, are you?

Mr Tunnicliffe just stares at him, the bottle poised

Well, go on—may as well pour yourself one now you've got the bottle in your hand.
Mr Tunnicliffe Thank you, sir. (*He pours, gratefully*)
Henry And pour one for me while you're at it.
Mr Tunnicliffe Yes, sir.

He pours another whisky. Henry goes to him to take it

Henry Catch your horse all right, then?
Mr Tunnicliffe Ah. Yes. Safe and sound.
Henry The *others* don't ride, do they?
Mr Tunnicliffe (*carefully*) Er . . . the others?
Henry Your partners. Tunnicliffe, Tunnicliffe and Tipthorpe.
Mr Tunnicliffe I'm sure I don't know.
Henry Well, surely you'd have noticed? You could hardly have missed three men arriving at the office on horseback. (*He chuckles*)
Mr Tunnicliffe (*deliberately vague*) I don't know what you mean. What partners? What office?

Henry wonders what the hell has got into Mr Tunnicliffe. He peers at him, closely

Henry Are you felling all right?
Mr Tunnicliffe Well . . . I am a little dizzy.
Henry I'm not surprised. Running around the meadows chasing a horse. Bound to make you dizzy, man of your age. (*He goes and sits on the sofa*)

Mr Tunnicliffe gathers his courage, with the help of a big swig of whisky

Mr Tunnicliffe But . . . I'm not . . . who you think I am.

Henry considers

Henry I beg your pardon?

Mr Tunnicliffe goes to Henry

Mr Tunnicliffe Well—who *do* you think I am?

Act II, Scene 1   41

Henry I *know* who you are, for God's sake! You're Tunnicliffe. Of Tunnicliffe, Tunnicliffe——
Mr Tunnicliffe No!
Henry No?
Mr Tunnicliffe No.
Henry Do you always go a bit funny when you've been in the saddle?

Mr Tunnicliffe sips his drink and sits L of Henry

Mr Tunnicliffe My name ... is Fishlock.

Henry gazes at him, motionless

Henry Fishlock?
Mr Tunnicliffe Yes. (*After a pause*) Albert Fishlock.
Henry Albert Fishlock. Good Lord ... (*After a pause*) I didn't know that.
Mr Tunnicliffe I *thought* it would be a surprise for you.
Henry It is. Oh, yes. Yes ... (*After a pause*) You must have wondered why I called you Tunnicliffe.

Mr Tunnicliffe smiles, nervously, nodding

Mr Tunnicliffe Well ... yes.
Henry You should have stopped me. You should have said, "For God's sake stop calling me Tunnicliffe when my name's Fishlock". (*He sips his whisky, thoughtfully*) Albert Fishlock. Well, well ...
Mr Tunnicliffe It's ... it's quite a nice name, isn't it?

Henry thinks about this

Henry Well ... yes. Yes, I suppose it is, really. Yes. I—I don't think *I'd* have minded being called Fishlock.
Mr Tunnicliffe It's unusual.
Henry Oh, yes. Chief Constable Henry Fishlock ... Has a ring to it.
Mr Tunnicliffe That's what *I* thought.

Quite a pause. Mr Tunnicliffe takes another nervous sip of his whisky

Can you guess what I do for a living?

Henry rises, impatiently, and paces away to C

Henry For heaven's sake, man—I *know* what you do for a living!
Mr Tunnicliffe Do you?
Henry Yes! You're a bloody solicitor!
Mr Tunnicliffe (*aggrieved*) No!
Henry (*controlling himself*) Ah. No. No, of course not. Silly of me. That was Tunnicliffe.
Mr Tunnicliffe Shall I tell you?
Henry No, no! Let me guess. Er ... slack wire act in a circus?
Mr Tunnicliffe No. But you're getting warm.
Henry Ring-master?
Mr Tunnicliffe Ah—no. Alas. Too short. I'm a vet.
Henry A *vet*?

Mr Tunnicliffe Yes—that's why I'm here. Mrs Winthrop is very worried about the pigs.
Henry How much whisky did you drink when you were in the cupboard?

Polly comes in DR. *She has now changed into a pleasant and revealing dress again. She goes to Henry*

Polly There we are! Is that better? (*She pirouettes to show herself off*)

Henry sees her and looks surprised. She sees Henry and looks surprised

Henry You've changed!
Polly So have you!
Henry What?
Polly I expect you found that other thing a bit too heavy.
Henry Why are you dressed like that?
Polly Do you like it? (*She twirls around, smiling*)
Henry No, I do *not* like it, as a matter of fact. I told you before. If you're one of his staff here I expect you to dress accordingly.

Polly is, naturally, taken aback by this apparent about-face

Polly That wasn't what you said just now!
Henry You'd better go and change.
Polly *Again*?
Henry Flat shoes, plain dress, white apron, little hat.
Polly But that's a *maid's* uniform!
Henry Precisely.
Polly Don't you mind that I'll be demeaning myself by dressing up in a uniform?
Henry As a Chief Constable, *I* don't object to dressing up in a uniform, so why should you? Off you go!
Polly (*bemused*) Off I go. Right you are, sir. (*Muttering as she goes*) Flat shoes, plain dress, white apron, little hat ... (*She turns*) Not all equal any more, then?
Henry What are you talking about?
Polly Not all equal. No. Change. Right you are, sir. Right away. Not all equal. ...

She goes out DR *muttering, at a loss to understand his change of heart*

Henry looks at Mr Tunnicliffe, balefully

Henry Fishlock ... (*No reply, so louder*) Fishlock!
Mr Tunnicliffe (*jumping*) Ah! H'm?
Henry That is your name, isn't it?
Mr Tunnicliffe Ah—yes. I'd forgotten for a moment.
Henry Shouldn't you be seeing to the pigs? They're probably dropping dead by the dozen out there.
Mr Tunnicliffe Yes. Of course. Mustn't neglect my duty. (*He starts to go, then stops*) But I'm in my suit.

Act II, Scene 1   43

Henry You should have thought of that before. If *my* name was Fishlock I wouldn't be wearing a suit. You'll have to borrow something. (*He takes the glass from Mr Tunnicliffe's hand, abruptly*) And you won't be wanting that.

He empties the remains of Mr Tunnicliffe's whisky into his own glass, hands the empty glass back to Mr Tunnicliffe and walks out to the front door

Mr Tunnicliffe looks, bleakly, at the empty glass, puts it down and follows Henry, miserably

Nora and Roger come in, through the archway, pushing a wicker laundry basket on castors

Roger (*unhappily*) I never thought I'd ever be pushing a window-cleaner about in a laundry basket . . .

They stop UC

Nora We could hardly leave him lying in Sycamore, could we? Suppose the Chief Constable had found him?
Roger But I've never done this sort of thing before. Trundling dead bodies in and out.
Nora Well, needs must when the devil drives.
Roger Yes—and you're the one doing the driving!
Nora You were glad enough of my help when you were searching for pleasure, Mr Featherstone.
Roger Yes, I know, but——
Nora Well, the wages of sin is death—and here it is! (*She indicates the laundry basket*)
Roger What are we going to do with him?
Nora We'll put him in the cow-shed.

   Sarah comes in through the archway. She has changed for dinner and has an air of mysterious rapture about her

Nora and Roger hastily stand side-by-side in front of the laundry basket to hide it from Sarah

Sarah Do you know—I think I've just seen a ghost.

Nora glances at the laundry basket, surprised

Nora Already? He can't have been *gone* very long.
Roger A ghost? What did he look like?
Sarah He seemed to be wearing a long cassock. Like a monk.
Roger Oh—*him!*
Sarah You mean *you*'ve seen him, too?
Roger Yes! He was here a moment ago.
Nora Who was?
Roger The Chief Constable—her brother!
Sarah Don't be silly, vicar. Why should Henry be wearing a cassock?
Roger *I* dunno. Dressing for dinner?

Sarah No, no. I'm sure it was Bernard.
Nora Who's Bernard?
Sarah My *other* brother.
Nora The one who fell off his tractor?
Sarah Yes. He joined a religious commune, you remember, so they might well have gone in for wearing cassocks.
Nora But he's dead!
Sarah Yes. (*Warmly*) Dear Bernard. I expect he's come back from heaven to see how we're all getting on. Why are you both standing in front of a laundry basket?
Roger I—I was helping Mrs Winthrop.
Nora The clergy are always very good about the dirty linen.
Sarah Where are you taking it?
Nora To the cow-shed.
Sarah Funny place to take the laundry.
Nora Yes. That's what *I* thought. But it's the van, you see.
Sarah The van?
Nora Laundry van. It parks outside the cow-shed and picks it up from there.
Sarah Why couldn't they bring the van up to the front door?
Nora They'd frighten the horse.
Sarah But the horse isn't *always* there, surely?
Nora Oh, no. Just this week. Come along, vicar!

Nora and Roger trundle the laundry basket out to the front door

Sarah watches them go, surprised

Bernard comes in from the archway

Bernard Ah! there you are, Sarah!

Sarah turns and sees what she believes to be a ghost. She gazes at him in awe

Sarah Good heavens...! I was right. It *is* you. I couldn't believe it.
Bernard I knew you'd be surprised. Do you think it suits me?
Sarah Oh, yes. It's quite nice. But it was very unfair of you, Bernard, to—to just... arrive like this. You know what a nervous sort of person I am. I might have fainted with the shock of seeing you.
Bernard Why? You never *used* to pass out when I came in the room.
Sarah No. Of course not. But that was *before*, wasn't it?
Bernard Before?
Sarah Well, it's not quite the same now!
Bernard Oh, you mean this thing? (*Indicating his cassock*)
Sarah I don't mean the way you're dressed, Bernard! I mean—(*with difficulty*)—well—you being... up there, and me still down here. (*She has a sudden doubt*) You *are* up there, aren't you? (*Pointing to heaven*) Oh, I don't mean *now*. Obviously, you're here now. But when you're not "visiting", you're... up there. Aren't you?

Bernard, who has been listening blankly, realizes what she means. Or what he thinks she means!

Act II, Scene 1

Bernard Ah! You mean in Scotland?
Sarah (*puzzled*) What?
Bernard Aren't you pleased to see me, Sarah?
Sarah Well . . . I would have liked a bit of warning.
Bernard Yes. I'm sorry about that. But you know what the post is like from up there.

Sarah looks puzzled

> *Jackie and Sally come in* DR. *They have now changed into short shorts and shirts (or whatever). They see Bernard*

Jackie (*to Sally*) He's here!
Sally Oh—yes.

They go to join the others

Jackie (*to Bernard*) We've been looking for you, sir.
Bernard Have you?
Sally We just wanted to apologise.
Bernard Apologize?
Jackie For screaming and running away when you were sitting on the sofa. I hope we didn't give you a shock.
Bernard Ah—so it was you two?
Jackie We didn't recognize you, you see.
Sally Dressed like that.
Bernard No wonder. You've never seen me before.

Jackie and Sally exchange a puzzled look

Sally Of course we'd seen you before.
Sarah My brother's only just arrived.
Jackie }
Sally } (*together*) What?!
Bernard How long have you both been working here?
Jackie About three months.
Sally On and off.
Bernard And what exactly do you do?

Jackie and Sally giggle, then try to be serious

Jackie Well . . . we look after the hens. Don't we, Sal?
Sally Yes! That's right—the hens!

They both make hen noises and giggle again. Bernard looks puzzled, naturally

> *Polly comes in* DR. *She is now back in her maid's uniform. She sees "Henry" is in his cassock again*

Polly I see you've slipped into that thing again. I don't blame you. It does get a bit chilly here in the evening.
Bernard Just a minute. Aren't you going to change?

Polly Pardon?
Bernard You're still in uniform.

Polly cannot believe her ears. Bernard smiles, benignly

Don't tell me you've forgotten what I said? About being equal.
Polly (*long-suffering*) Oh—that ...
Bernard These young ladies work here as well, you know, and *they* aren't in uniform, are they?
Polly No, but you said——
Bernard (*firm but gentle*) No argument now. All equal. Remember? Go and change.
Polly All equal. Go and change. Right you are, sir. Right away, sir. All equal.
Bernard That's the idea!
Polly Yes, sir. Thank you, sir. All equal, sir. (*As she goes*) I wish you'd make up your bloody mind ...!

She goes out DR

Sarah is appalled by her behaviour

Sarah Polly! I shall go and have a word with that girl. (*She goes towards the door*) She has no right to speak to a ghost like that.

Sarah goes out after Polly

Bernard looks bewildered. Jackie and Sally look alarmed

Jackie Who's she talking about?
Bernard (*modestly*) Me, I think.
Jackie *You*?
Bernard Yes.
Sally You're not a ghost, are you?

Bernard shrugs, helplessly

Jackie and Sally scream and run away into the garden

Nora and Roger come back in from the front door, pushing the laundry basket, desperately

Nora Why didn't you make sure it was all clear?
Roger *I* didn't know the Chief Constable was out there.
Nora Well, hurry up—before he sees us!

They come in with the laundry basket. They do not see Bernard. He watches their approach in some surprise. Finally, they see him, react and stop. They look back the way they have come and then at Bernard in disbelief

How did you get in here?
Bernard (*indicating the way he came*) From out there.
Nora But just now you were out there! (*Indicating the other direction*) Talking to the man in the suit.
Bernard No, no. I was in here talking to my sister.

Act II, Scene 1

Nora and Roger are bewildered

For some reason she seems to think that I'm a ghost. (*He chuckles*) Sarah always did have a tendency to flights of fancy. Is this good lady your wife?
Nora (*outraged*) Of course I'm not his wife! I'm Mrs Winthrop—remember? I work here!
Bernard Ah. My mistake. I'm so sorry. Jumping to conclusions. You looked so united pushing the basket.
Nora The vicar was just helping me take the laundry out to the cow-shed.
Bernard It seems awfully heavy ...
Nora Yes—well, there is a bit more in the basket than usual. Come on, vicar—let's get it out of here!
Bernard But why were you taking the laundry out to the cow-shed?
Nora So the van wouldn't frighten the horse.
Bernard Horse?
Nora Big black horse. At the front door.
Bernard What's a horse doing at the front door?
Nora He left it there when he arrived.
Bernard Who did?
Nora The man in the suit.
Bernard What man?
Nora The one who was in the cupboard with a bottle of whisky.
Bernard Ah—yes! I remember him! What exactly was he doing in the cupboard?
Nora Reading the gas meter.
Bernard With a bottle of whisky?
Nora Well, it's very cold in there.
Bernard But he must have finished by now.
Nora The whisky?
Bernard Reading the gas meter!
Nora Ah—yes.
Bernard So that's all right, then, isn't it?
Nora Is it?
Bernard Well, now he'll go home on the horse.
Nora Very likely.
Bernard And the laundry van isn't due until Friday, so there's no need to put the basket in the cow-shed.
Nora Ah. No. I suppose not. Come on, then, vicar! Let's get it out of here!
Bernard I'll give you a hand.
Roger No!!
Bernard (*surprised*) What?
Roger You'll get your cassock caught.

Bernard smiles, ecumenically

Bernard We may be on different sides of the ecclesiastical fence but I think we can unite in the moving of a laundry basket. Come along, vicar!

He and Roger start to push

Polly comes in DR, *having changed out of her uniform*

Nora (*seeing her*) Why are you dressed like that?
Polly He *wants* me dressed like this! (*She glares at Bernard*)
Bernard (*crossing to her*) Ah—yes. That's more like it.
Polly Your sister's carrying on like a thing possessed out there. Thinks she's seen a ghost.
Bernard I'd better go and speak to her. Sorry, vicar, but you'll have to manage without me.
Roger Thank God for that . . .!

Nora elbows him, and he doubles up in pain

Bernard (*to Polly*) My sister seems to think I've come from heaven.

He goes off DR

Nora remonstrates with Polly

Nora I told you to check that all the rooms were empty.
Polly They *were* empty.
Nora Sycamore wasn't!
Polly (*crossing to Nora*) Of course it was. The bank manager was in Sycamore and he went off on a bicycle.
Nora Exactly—on the window-cleaner's bicycle!
Polly Yes.
Nora And remember what happened to the window-cleaner, Polly?
Polly He fell off his ladder.
Nora Exactly! So he probably hit his head on something and staggered into Sycamore to have a lie-down!
Polly I expect he felt faint. Oh, poor thing. But he'll soon be all right. Did you tell him to go?
Nora I couldn't.
Polly Why not?
Nora Because he's dead!
Polly *Dead?* (*She cannot believe her ears*) You mean there's a dead window-cleaner lying down in Sycamore?
Nora Well . . . no. Not any more. We couldn't just leave him there, could we?
Polly Well, where is he now?
Nora In there! (*Indicating the basket*)
Polly (*appalled*) In *there*?!

Henry walks in from the front door with his empty whisky glass

They all look at him in surprise, then turn their heads in unison to look the way Bernard has gone, then back to Henry again. Hastily, they sit in a row on top of the laundry basket, inadvertently taking up the poses of the three wise monkeys. Henry surveys them in silence for a moment, then chuckles

Henry Hear no evil, see no evil, speak no evil.

Act II, Scene 1   49

Polly whispers to Roger
Polly He's changed again. ...
Henry peers at them. They shift, uncomfortably
Henry Have you seen my sister anywhere?
Nora (*looking puzzled*) Couldn't you find her, then?
Henry When?
Nora When you were out there. (*Indicating the way Bernard has gone*)
Henry (*puzzled*) Out there? Last time *I* saw her she was in the garden.
Nora tries to work this out
Nora You mean she saw the ghost in the *garden*?
Henry What ghost?
Nora The ghost your sister saw!
Henry Are you feeling all right?
Nora I was until a moment ago ...!
Henry I don't know what's the matter with you three. Why do you keep trundling the laundry basket in and out?
Nora Well, why do *you* keep changing your clothes?
Henry I beg your pardon?
Nora And you don't half move fast. One minute you're out there, then you're in here, then you're out there, and now you're in here again!
Henry (*smiling, sagely*) Ah—well, you have to be speedy in the Force. As a Chief Constable I have to be one step ahead of my men. (*He executes a neat foot movement*)
Nora At this rate, you must be about two *miles* ahead of them!
Henry (*crossing to the drinks cupboard*) Perhaps *you* could find my sister for me, Mrs Winthrop? She's probably dozed off in her room. (*He pours himself another whisky*)
Nora (*reluctantly*) Oh, very well. (*She gets off the laundry basket and turns back to Roger*) You look after the laundry. (*She heads for the archway*)
Henry You needn't worry. The laundry won't disappear. (*He chuckles*)
Nora I wish it would!

She goes, quickly, through the archway

Henry Well, vicar—I expect you're ready for another pint of sherry. (*He picks up the sherry bottle*)
Roger A small one would be welcome.
Henry Well, there isn't any. (*He holds up the empty bottle and looks at Roger, suspiciously*) Have you been helping yourself?
Roger No, of course not!
Henry It's all the same to me. I'm having whisky. I won't offer *you* whisky, vicar. I always think sherry's quite sufficient for the clergy. Start delving into spirits and we'll find sex creeping into your sermons. You'll find another bottle out there.
Roger There's really no need——

Henry (*crossing to Roger*) Of course there's need. My sister's very fond of a glass or two of sherry. Go and get it, there's a good chap.
Roger Oh—very well. (*To Polly*) You look after the laundry.
Henry You all seem very concerned about the dirty linen. (*To Roger*) Off you go. It's through there on the left. You can't miss it. I don't expect *you* need radar to find a bottle of sherry.

Roger stumbles out, nervously DR

Polly looks at Henry, thoughtfully

Polly You're a fast mover, I'll say that for you.
Henry I beg your pardon?
Polly You must have had plenty of practice getting your clothes on and off. . . .

Debbie comes in from the front door, to C. *Apart from the farmer's hat, she is now only wearing bra and pants*

Henry gapes, aghast

Debbie You've never going to believe what's happened!
Henry (*going to her, astonished*) I can *see* what's happened! Why have you taken your clothes off?
Debbie He told me to!
Henry Who did?
Debbie The little man in the suit.
Henry Mr Tunnicliffe? He was supposed to be seeing to the pigs.
Debbie Well, he told me to take them off.
Polly And you *did*?
Debbie Well, I always take them off when I'm told.
Henry You took your clothes off—in the garden—in front of Mr Tunnicliffe?
Debbie Yes! And then *he* put them on!
Henry I knew there was something strange about that man. . . .
Debbie He said he needed them to see to the pigs because he didn't want to spoil his suit.
Henry Ah—yes! Of course. Well, you'd better go and get something else on. What will my sister say if she sees you like that? (*To Polly*) And you, too! I thought I told you to go and change?

Polly gazes at him in disbelief

Polly I have changed!
Henry You haven't changed anything that *I* can see.

Polly goes to him

Polly (*losing control*) You're the one who's changed! You keep changing your mind!
Henry (*appalled*) Have you gone mad?
Polly No, but I reckon *you* have!
Henry Get that dress off at once!

Act II, Scene 2

Polly All right, Chief Constable! You asked for it!

Having reached the end of her tether. Polly proceeds to take off her dress in front of Henry. He cannot believe what is happening! She has removed her dress and is standing there in the full glory of bra and pants, and is about to remove them as well, when . . .

    Sarah comes in DR. *At the same time, Jackie and Sally come in through the archway*

Sarah reacts, appalled, at seeing her brother with two very scantily-clad young ladies. Jackie and Sally look on, amused

Sarah Henry!!

Henry, Polly and Debbie turn and see Sarah

    And at that moment, the lid of the laundry basket opens and the figure of a man emerges like Lazarus and, without noticing anybody, races out to the front door

The girls all scream and everybody is watching the man disappearing as there is a Black-out, and——

    the CURTAIN *falls*

SCENE 2

The same. A little later

Henry is walking, briskly, in from the garden, carrying a shotgun. Sarah is following, anxiously

Sarah Henry! Henry—what *are* you going to do?
Henry (*casually*) I'm going to shoot the vicar.
Sarah Why?
Henry Because he's not a vicar at all.
Sarah You can't shoot someone just because they're not a vicar.
Henry You'll want to shoot him, too, when I tell you what I heard from the man in the laundry basket.
Sarah Oh—you managed to catch up with him, then? Who was he?
Henry The window-cleaner.
Sarah The one who fell off his ladder?
Henry Yes. (*He examines his shotgun*)
Sarah (*happily*) Oh, good! He's all right, then . . .
Henry We had a little talk and then he went home. I've never seen a window-cleaner on horseback before . . .
Sarah Horseback?
Henry There was a horse outside the front door. You remember. Big black horse. About seventeen hands. He went home on that.
Sarah Why?

Henry (*impatiently*) Because the bank manager had taken his bicycle.
Sarah But the horse didn't belong to the window-cleaner. The horse belonged to the man in the suit.
Henry Yes, that's right. Fishlock.
Sarah Is *that* his name?
Henry It is now!

Roger comes in, DR

Roger I'm sorry I've been so long. I couldn't find the sherry. (*He sees Henry with the shotgun and gives a nervous laugh*) Aaaah! Going after a brace of pheasant?
Henry (*eyeing him, balefully*) No, Mr Featherstone. I leave pheasant to the amateur. (*He raises his gun, thoughtfully*)

Sarah clutches at Henry's arm, fearful of what he is about to do

Sarah Now Henry dear—don't do anything rash ...
Henry While you were out there searching for sherry certain things have come to light.
Roger H-have they?
Sarah (*to Roger, nodding*) Yes, they have ...
Henry Everything is now ... out in the open.
Roger I-is it?
Sarah Yes, it is ...
Roger Ah. I didn't know that.
Henry (*ominously*) I now know exactly what's been going on here.

Roger looks fearful

Roger You do?
Sarah Yes, he does ...
Henry That's why I'm loading this thing—*Mister* Featherstone.
Roger I-I-I-I'll go and see if the sherry's out there.

He disappears like a frightened rabbit through the archway

Henry (*chuckling*) I always like to give villains a few yards start.
Sarah I can't think what the window-cleaner can have told you to make you think of shooting the vicar.

Henry takes his sister's hand, sympathetically, and leads her to the sofa. They sit, side-by-side

Henry Sarah—I don't know if I should tell you this. I know how upset you'll be. A woman of your sensitivity and high moral values ...
Sarah What *are* you talking about?
Henry I told you I thought there was something fishy going on here, didn't I?
Sarah Henry, do get on with it.
Henry Very well. Be brave, Sarah. Be brave. You see ... ever since Mrs Winthrop took over as housekeeper here, this place has been used as ... as a house of ill-repute.

Act II, Scene 2   53

Sarah (*blankly, after a pause*) What does that mean?
Henry You know very well what it means!
Sarah No, I don't.
Henry It means that Polly and the other girls aren't here for the *farming*——
Sarah Then what *are* they here for?
Henry (*impatiently*) They're here for the——(*He checks himself in time*) I'm trying to be as delicate as I can, Sarah. Mrs Winthrop has been running a . . . a house of sin.
Sarah *Here?*
Henry Yes.
Sarah Good heavens—how exciting! I've never slept in a house of sin before.
Henry (*astonished*) You're not shocked?
Sarah Henry, I do know that sort of thing goes on. (*She laughs*) Call yourself a policeman? Vice under your very nose and you didn't even find out about it.
Henry I *did* find out about it!
Sarah Only when a dead window-cleaner appeared out of a laundry basket and told you. (*Thoughtfully*) So that's why those girls had taken their clothes off. No wonder Bernard came back from the grave!
Henry What?
Sarah (*mystically*) I've just been talking to Bernard.
Henry (*remembering*) Good heavens! Is he here already? I forgot to tell you he was arriving.
Sarah You mean you *knew* he was coming down from up there?
Henry Yes, of course! Isn't it splendid?
Sarah (*puzzled*) How did you know?
Henry Mr Tunnicliffe told me.
Sarah (*a little put out*) But how did *he* know?
Henry (*patiently*) Sarah, he's a solicitor. They're paid to know. That's why he's here.
Sarah You mean Mr Tunnicliffe's here, as well?
Henry Yes. Of course. He's Fishlock.
Sarah How can he be Tunnicliffe *and* Fishlock?
Henry Don't ask me! (*He gets up and starts to go, carrying his shotgun*)
Sarah Where are you going?
Henry I told you. I'm going to shoot the vicar.
Sarah But if you shoot the vicar, what will you do with him?
Henry (*casually*) I'll put him in the laundry basket.

He goes out through the archway

Sarah (*reacting in alarm*) Henry, dear, you mustn't do that . . .! (*She is about to follow Henry*)

But Nora comes in from the garden, expecting to find Bernard still there

Nora I can't find her anywhere——(*She sees Sarah*) Oh, there you are! The Chief Constable was looking for you. Did he find you?
Sarah Yes, he certainly did! (*Saucily*) You naughty old thing . . .!

She giggles and goes out after Henry, hardly able to control her laughter

Nora looks after her in surprise, then remembers the window-cleaner and goes quickly to the laundry basket. She prepares to push the heavy load on her own, lifting her skirt a little and bending down to get greater purchase. To her surprise, the basket moves easily and she nearly falls. Puzzled, she carefully lifts the lid half an inch or so to peer inside. Not able to see, she opens the lid fully and looks inside. Aghast at finding the basket empty, she slams the lid quickly and sits on top of the basket.

Mr Tunnicliffe comes in from the front door. He is now wearing the boots, corduroy trousers and shirt that Debbie was wearing (facsimiles)

Mr Tunnicliffe Somebody seems to have stolen my steed.
Nora (*her mind elsewhere*) I beg your pardon, dear?
Mr Tunnicliffe I left my horse securely tethered outside, but it seems to have disappeared.
Nora That's not the only thing that's disappeared! (*Seeing him*) Why are you wearing Debbie's clothes?
Mr Tunnicliffe I had to see to the pigs. (*He smiles, conspiratorily*) My name is Fishlock. I'm a veterinary surgeon. Remember?
Nora What? (*Remembering*) Oh, yes! Good. Well done, dear. But have you seen the window-cleaner?

Mr Tunnicliffe glances at the windows

Mr Tunnicliffe Your windows don't appear to be in need of attention.
Nora No, but the window-cleaner is! He was lying about in here and now he's disappeared.
Mr Tunnicliffe (*moving to below the sofa, thoughtfully*) I don't know how I'm going to get back to the village without my horse . . .

Roger comes in from the garden, furtively, to R of Nora

Roger Has he gone?
Nora (*looking at the laundry basket*) Yes, he has! And I can't understand it.
Roger Which way did he go?
Nora I only wish I knew!
Mr Tunnicliffe I don't suppose you've seen a loose horse in the garden?

Roger turns to look at Mr Tunnicliffe, irritated by the interruption

Roger What?
Mr Tunnicliffe I've lost my horse.
Nora Somebody must have moved him!
Roger The horse?
Nora The window-cleaner!
Roger But he was in the laundry basket.
Mr Tunnicliffe A window-cleaner in a laundry basket? How very singular . . . (*He sits on the sofa*)
Nora Well, he's not in there now!

Act II, Scene 2   55

Roger What? (*He throws back the lid of the laundry basket. He looks aghast and shuts it again, staring at Nora*) He's gone!
Nora That's what I told you, Mr Featherstone.
Mr Tunnicliffe What was the window-cleaner doing in the laundry basket?
Roger Oh, shut up! (*To Nora*) Where can he have gone to?
Nora *I* don't know! But he can't have gone far, the state he was in.

Jackie and Sally run in through the archway

Jackie Mrs Winthrop! You'll never guess what *we* saw!
Sally We saw a ghost!
Nora What?
Jackie Right here in this room!
Nora A ghost?
Sally Well, she said it was a ghost.
Nora Who did?
Jackie The Chief Constable's sister.
Nora You don't want to believe anything *she* says!
Sally But we saw him!
Jackie In here! Over there!
Sally And then we saw something else!
Nora Oh, yes?
Jackie A man!
Sally In there!
Nora In where?
Jackie In the basket.
Nora *This* basket?
Jackie ⎫
Sally ⎬ (*together*) Yes!

Nora and Roger exchange a quick look

Nora ⎫
Roger ⎬ (*together*) You *saw* him?
Jackie ⎫
Sally ⎬ (*together*) Yes!
Jackie He got out of the basket and ran out through the front door!
Nora You mean he was alive?
Jackie Well, he went out of here fast enough.
Roger (*relaxing*) Oh, well, that's all right, then! (*To Nora*) He wasn't dead, after all.
Nora So now we don't have to worry, do we?
Roger (*remembering something*) Oh, yes, we do . . .!
Nora Do we?
Roger Yes! The Chief Constable's racing around with a shotgun!
Jackie ⎫
Sally ⎬ (*together*) A gun!
Mr Tunnicliffe (*miserably*) She did *say* I might not get out of here alive . . .
Nora (*to Roger*) Don't be silly, dear. Why should the Chief Constable be carrying firearms?

Roger Because he's found out what's been going on here!
Nora (*appalled*) Oh, no!
Roger Oh, yes!

Bernard comes in from the front door

Sally and Jackie see him and react in horror

Jackie Look—it's him!
Sally He's back again!

They scream and run out into the garden

Bernard smiles, tolerantly, at Roger

Bernard I can't think what I've done to frighten them.
Mr Tunnicliffe (*not daring to look*) You aren't going to shoot me, are you?
Bernard Why on earth should I shoot you? (*He sees Mr Tunnicliffe's apparel*) Good heavens!
Mr Tunnicliffe What? (*He sees Bernard for the first time and is equally astonished*) Good heavens...!

Bernard crosses to L of the sofa, looking thoughtfully at Mr Tunnicliffe in Debbie's clothes. Nora turns to Roger, sceptically, and whispers to him

Nora You see? He's not carrying a gun!
Roger Don't you be too sure. He'll have hidden it under his skirt!
Mr Tunnicliffe (*gazing at Bernard*) Why are you dressed like that?
Bernard Well, why are *you* dressed like *that*?
Mr Tunnicliffe (*angrily*) Because I'm a veterinary surgeon! You told me to see to the pigs!
Bernard A veterinary surgeon? (*He turns to Nora*) Mrs Winthrop...?

Nora fawns, nervously

Nora Oh, I didn't mean any harm, sir. But there are so many lonely men about. And this is such a big house. It seemed such a shame to waste all those empty rooms. It was just ... innocent fun.
Bernard (*totally lost*) What are you talking about?
Nora Well... (*she looks around, furtively*) ... "you-know-what".
Bernard (*blankly*) You-know-what?
Nora Yes! That's why *he*'s pretending to be a vet, and *he*'s pretending to be a vicar.
Bernard (*turning to Mr Tunnicliffe*) You mean you're *not* a veterinary surgeon?
Mr Tunnicliffe (*bewildered*) Well... I...
Bernard (*to Roger*) And you're not a vicar?
Roger I'm afraid not...
Bernard You *look* like a vicar. (*To Mr Tunnicliffe*) And you're wearing boots!
Nora Well, you're wearing a cassock, but it doesn't mean that you're the Pope, does it?
Bernard I don't understand...

Act II, Scene 2   57

Mr Tunnicliffe Neither do I . . .
Nora It's all because of "you-know-what"!
Bernard (*completely bewildered*) I don't know what you're talking about.
Mr Tunnicliffe Neither do I . . .!
Nora (*surprised*) You—you don't?
Bernard I don't even know what "you-know-what" *is*!

Nora turns to glare at Roger

Sarah comes in through the archway

Sarah I can't find Henry out there. He must be hiding from me. (*She sees Bernard and speaks in hushed, reverent tones*) Ah . . . you're still here . . .! How splendid! (*To Nora*) I told you I'd seen a ghost, didn't I?
Nora What are you talking about?
Sarah Oh—perhaps *you* can't see him! He's standing over there. (*Indicating Bernard*)
Nora Of course I can see him! And he looks pretty solid to me.
Sarah (*with a saucy giggle*) Have you told him about . . . "you-know-what"?
Nora I thought he already *knew*——
Roger (*wildly*) He does! He does know! He said so! Didn't you? That's why you've been running around with a shotgun!
Bernard A shotgun?
Sarah Oh, don't be silly, vicar. It was *Henry* with the shotgun.

Everybody looks confused

Nora I beg your pardon?
Mr Tunnicliffe What are you talking about?
Sarah This isn't Henry. This is my other brother—Bernard.
Nora Well, he looks just like him!
Sarah Of course he does. Bernard and Henry are identical twins.
Mr Tunnicliffe *I* never knew that, and I'm their solicitor . . .
Nora But you said your brother Bernard was dead.
Sarah (*smiling, delightedly*) Yes—exactly! (*She indicates Bernard*) And he's over there . . .
Nora You . . . you mean he really *is* a . . .?
Sarah Yes! I told you! (*To Bernard*) I was telling Mrs Winthrop that you're only visiting . . . from the other place. (*To Nora*) I've never met one before, have you?
Nora (*gazing at Sarah*) No, but I've met one now all right! (*She goes to Bernard*) It's not true, is it?
Bernard Oh, yes.
Nora It *is*?
Bernard Yes.
Nora You really *have* come from . . . up there?
Bernard Yes. Of course. I came down on the early train.
Nora From heaven?
Bernard From Scotland.
Nora }
Sarah } (*together*) Scotland?!

Bernard Yes.
Sarah You mean you're *not* a ghost?
Bernard (*laughing*) Of course I'm not a ghost, Sarah.
Nora (*to Sarah*) There you are, you see!
Sarah But, Bernard, you fell off your tractor in the Orkneys!
Bernard More than once, but it wasn't fatal.
Mr Tunnicliffe (*to Sarah*) That's what I came here to tell you.
Roger (*to Nora, quietly*) That means there are *two* of them about!
Nora (*to Roger, quietly*) Yes—and the other one's the one with the gun!

Roger starts to go

Where are *you* going?
Roger To practise the Lord's Prayer.

He goes out through the archway

Nora Well, wait for me! (*She starts to follow him*)
Bernard (*puzzled*) Mrs Winthrop . . .

She stops

I'm a little confused.
Mr Tunnicliffe You're not the only one . . .
Bernard Why is my brother carrying a shotgun?
Nora I expect he's here for the grouse shooting. (*She starts to go again*)
Bernard Mrs Winthrop!

She stops

It's too early for grouse.
Nora Is it? I didn't know that. (*She tries again*)
Bernard Mrs Winthrop.

She stops

You seem very anxious to leave us.
Nora Yes—I want to get out of the firing line!

She scuttles out, quickly, before he can stop her again

Sarah (*going towards Bernard*) Really, Bernard—you might have told me you weren't a ghost. What *will* Mrs Winthrop think of me?
Bernard Mrs Winthrop seems to have other things on her mind at the moment. I'd better go and find Henry before he starts shooting at her.

He goes out into the garden

Mr Tunnicliffe (*miserably*) If only I could find my horse, then I could go home . . .

Polly and Debbie come in DR. *They are now dressed in short skirts and jackets and are ready to leave. They move to* L *of the sofa, on their way to the front door*

Act II, Scene 2   59

Sarah Where are you going?
Debbie We're not staying in this place!
Polly No! Changing my clothes every five minutes is one thing, but dead window-cleaners climbing out of laundry baskets is another.
Debbie So we're going down to the road to hitch a lift home.
Sarah You're not going to hitch a lift dressed like *that*?
Polly Dressed like this we'll have them queuing up! (*She giggles*)
Sarah But you can't go without telling Mrs Winthrop. You'll leave her short-staffed.
Polly Well, it's not exactly business as usual at the moment, is it?
Debbie What happened to the man in the basket?
Sarah Oh. He went home on a horse.
Mr Tunnicliffe (*looking up*) A horse?
Sarah Yes. I'm afraid so.
Mr Tunnicliffe That was *my* horse! Now I'll *never* get home ... (*He cries*)
Sarah Henry had quite a chat with him.
Debbie The horse?
Sarah The window-cleaner. He told Henry all about "you-know-what"! (*She giggles*)
Polly You mean you *know* what's been going on here?
Sarah Oh, yes. (*Joyfully*) A house of sin ...! That's why Henry's so upset.
Polly *You* don't seem very upset.
Sarah Why should I be? I'm delighted! I think it's all rather exciting! (*Remembering*) Oh, good heavens! Bernard doesn't know. I must go and tell him all about it!

She goes out into the garden, enjoying the prospect hugely, calling as she goes

Bernard ...! Bernard ...!

Mr Tunnicliffe is wiping his eyes, miserably

Mr Tunnicliffe I'll never trust a window-cleaner again ...

Polly notices what Mr Tunnicliffe is wearing

Polly Why have you got Debbie's clothes on? You were in a suit when you were chasing the horse.
Mr Tunnicliffe I was told to see to the pigs ...

A gunshot from outside, off L. *They all jump in surprise*

All Aaah!!

Mr Tunnicliffe leaps up and runs across towards the laundry basket, crying bitterly

Polly What was that?
Mr Tunnicliffe The Chief Constable!
Debbie Shooting?
Mr Tunnicliffe Yes!

Polly What's he shooting at?
Mr Tunnicliffe I think he's shooting at *me*! (*He lifts the lid of the laundry basket, steps inside and pulls it down after him*)

Polly and Debbie look on, astonished

Debbie Poor little chap. Why should the Chief Constable want to shoot him?

Henry marches in through the archway, carrying his shotgun

Polly and Debbie hastily sit on top of the laundry basket and try to appear casual

Henry Any sign of the vicar?
Polly Is *that* who you're looking for?
Henry Yes. I want to have a word with him. Seen him anywhere?
Debbie No. *He*'s not in here.

She and Polly giggle

Henry Right. (*He starts to go towards the front door, then stops and returns to them*) Why are you sitting on a laundry basket? (*Suspiciously*) I hope you're not hiding the vicar in there.
Polly No—of course not!
Debbie (*quietly*) No. Not the *vicar* ...

She and Polly giggle again

Henry What?
Polly We put sheets and pillow cases in here, not clergymen.
Henry Then I'm sure you'll have no objection to my inspecting the dirty linen. (*He waves his gun at them*) Off you get! Come on—off!

Reluctantly, the girls get off the laundry basket. Henry stands with his gun at the ready

Right—open it up!

Polly opens the lid of the laundry basket. Mr Tunnicliffe's head appears. He is still crying. He sees Henry's gun, raises his hands quickly and cries even more

Mr Tunnicliffe Don't shoot! I can explain!

Henry cannot believe his eyes

Henry Tunnicliffe! (*Then, warmly*) Mr dear fellow ...
Polly
Debbie } (*together, moved*) Aaaaah ...

Mr Tunnicliffe's tears subside a little

Henry I don't know what's the matter with you, Tunnicliffe. I think you're in need of therapy. First of all you hide in a cupboard, then in a laundry basket. Have you been drinking again?
Mr Tunnicliffe I wish I had ...!

Act II, Scene 2

Henry (*casually*) Well, if you see the vicar—let me know. All right?

He closes the lid of the laundry basket on the astonished occupant and walks briskly out to the front door

Polly I think he's going to shoot the vicar!
Debbie Don't be daft. He said he wanted to talk to him.
Polly With a shotgun! I'd better find Mrs Winthrop and tell her what's happening.

She goes out through the archway

Roger comes in from the garden, looking about, nervously, to see if the coast is clear

Debbie Oh, there you are! The Chief Constable's looking for you!
Roger Yes, I know . . .!
Debbie I'll go and tell him you're here. (*She starts to go*)
Roger No!! Don't do that!
Debbie He only wants to talk to you.

Debbie runs out to the front door, calling

Chief Constable . . .!
Roger Oh, my God!

Roger looks about in panic, wondering where to hide. He sees the laundry basket and hastens to it. He throws back the lid to reveal Mr Tunnicliffe. He is still crying

Mr Tunnicliffe Go away! This basket is occupied.
Roger Come on—out you get!
Mr Tunnicliffe But I was here first!
Roger Never mind that. Come on—out!

Roger pulls him, protesting, out of the laundry basket and steps into it himself, leaving Mr Tunnicliffe dithering, uncertainly

Mr Tunnicliffe But what am *I* going to do?
Roger You'll think of something. (*He sinks down into the basket, closing the lid after him*)

Mr Tunnicliffe hears voices approaching in the garden

Mr Tunnicliffe Oh, dear—here I go again . . .! (*He goes towards the cupboard, sees the bottle of whisky, collects it neatly as he passes and disappears into the cupboard, cheering up considerably. He closes the door behind him*)

The telephone rings. But there is nobody there to answer it. It stops as somebody picks up the extension in another part of the house

Bernard comes briskly in from the garden, with Sarah following him. He is looking far from pleased

Sarah I don't know what you're making such a fuss about. I wish I hadn't told you now. I thought you'd be pleased.

Bernard Pleased? I go to the Orkneys to live off the land and be nearer to God, and the minute I've gone my house becomes a den of vice!
Sarah (*smiling*) I thought it was rather exciting . . .
Bernard Well, it shouldn't be!

Polly comes in through the archway and crosses to behind the laundry basket. She bends down to speak to it

Polly You're wanted on the telephone.

Bernard and Sarah exchange an astonished look. They have not seen someone speaking to a laundry basket before. Polly casts a nervous smile in their direction, and tries again

You're wanted on the telephone.

The laundry basket is unmoved. Polly looks at the others again, and gives another embarrassed smile. Then she opens the lid of the laundry basket

You're wanted on the——

Roger's head appears, furtively

Roger What do you want?

Bernard and Sarah cannot believe their eyes. Nor can Polly

Polly What are *you* doing in there? I left that other chap in this basket.
Roger I should try the cupboard, if I were you. (*He sinks from sight, pulling the lid closed after him*)

Bernard and Sarah exchange a dazed look. Polly goes to the cupboard and knocks on the door. The cupboard door creaks open and Mr Tunnicliffe peers out, a little cross at being disturbed

Mr Tunnicliffe What do you want?
Polly Telephone!
Mr Tunnicliffe Well, can't you take a message?
Polly They said it was important.
Mr Tunnicliffe (*reluctantly*) Oh, very well. (*He comes out of the cupboard, carrying the bottle of whisky, and sees Bernard and Sarah watching him. He smiles, self-consciously*) I'm wanted on the telephone. I'll . . . I'll take it out here so as not to disturb you.

He scuttles out, quickly, through the archway

Polly is about to follow him, but hangs back for a moment

Polly I see you're back in the blanket again, Chief Constable!
Bernard No, no—*I'm* not the Chief Constable.
Polly Pardon?
Bernard I'm his twin brother—Bernard.
Polly But I thought you were dead.
Sarah So did I! (*She gives Bernard a disapproving look*)

Act II, Scene 2   63

Polly Twins, eh? I wondered why you kept changing your clothes . . .

She goes out through the archway

Bernard drifts, thoughtfully, below the sofa

Bernard It was never like this in the Orkneys . . .

Jackie and Sally come in from the garden and see Bernard in his cassock. They scream

Jackie Aah! There he is again!

They start to go, terrified

Sarah It's all right, girls. There's no need to be frightened. It's only my brother.

Jackie and Sally come in, cautiously, to L of Sarah, their eyes on Bernard

Jackie We thought he was a ghost.
Bernard Well, we all make mistakes. Don't we, Sarah?
Sarah (*glaring at him*) Yes, we certainly do!
Sally I've never seen a Chief Constable dressed like that before . . .
Sarah Oh, this isn't Henry! This is my *other* brother—Bernard.
Sally Well, he looks just like him.
Sarah Of course he does. They're twins.
Jackie Oh, I see! There's two of you! Well, now we know, eh, Sal?
Bernard Yes. And now *I* know, too.
Jackie Sorry?
Bernard What's been going on here while I've been in the Orkneys.

Jackie and Sally look at Sarah

Sarah I'm afraid I told him.
Jackie
Sally } (*together*) What?!
Bernard (*grimly*) And I shall have a very strong word with Mrs Winthrop about this, I can tell you!
Sarah No, Bernard, you mustn't do that——
Bernard Which way did she go?
Sarah Oh—er—*that* way. (*Indicating the door* DR)
Bernard Right. (*He starts to go*)
Sarah You can't blame Mrs Winthrop. She was only thinking of other people's pleasure.
Bernard Yes! That's the trouble!

He goes out DR

Sarah (*going to the sofa*) Bernard always was such a dreadful spoilsport . . . (*She sits down*)

Debbie comes racing in through the front door

Debbie The laundry van's coming up the road!

Nora comes sailing in through the archway. She is now wearing her coat and hat, ready for the off

Sarah Mrs Winthrop! Where are you going?
Nora I'm not staying here to be shot at!
Debbie The laundry van's coming up the road, Mrs Winthrop!
Nora He's not due till Friday. Oh, well—never mind, eh? Perhaps he'll give me a lift. Right, girls—get the basket outside!
Jackie Can't the laundry man get it himself?
Nora We can give him a hand, can't we? Come on! Many hands make light work.

Chattering like magpies, Debbie, Jackie and Sally start to push the laundry basket out

Sally Oo, this is a bit heavy, isn't it?
Debbie Oh, for heaven's sake, Sally—push!
Jackie Come on, you two!

The girls disappear out to the front door, pushing the laundry basket (and its occupant)

Henry comes in through the archway, carrying his shotgun. He sees Nora with her coat and hat on

Henry Going somewhere, Mrs Winthrop?

Nora jumps, nervously, and puts her hands up above her head

Nora Don't shoot! I can explain! I thought it was all for the best.
Henry All for the best? I'll deal with you later. (*He crosses to* L *of the sofa*) Any sign of the vicar, Sarah? I can't think *where* he's hiding himself.
Sarah (*remembering*) *I* can! Oh, dear ...! (*She starts to laugh*)
Henry What's the matter?
Sarah Oh, dear. Oh, dear ...!

Polly comes running in through the archway

Polly Mrs Winthrop! The laundry van's outside and—— (*She stops when she sees that the basket has gone*) What's happened to the laundry basket?
Sarah (*smiling, knowingly*) It's just going ...
Polly What?!

A loud cheer outside from the girls as they succeed in getting the laundry basket into the van. Henry looks towards the noise

Henry What's going on out there?
Nora The girls are just helping to load the laundry basket.
Polly (*going to Sarah*) But surely that means that——?
Sarah (*nodding*) Yes!

Polly sits beside Sarah on the sofa and they laugh

Henry What's so funny about a laundry basket?

Act II, Scene 2   65

Sarah (*trying to keep a straight face*) Nothing, Henry. Until they open it up. Then they're going to find more than they bargained for!

She and Polly laugh, helplessly

Mr Tunnicliffe walks in through the archway. He is looking a little dazed, walking like a man in a dream. He is still carrying the bottle of whisky

Henry (*looking at him*) Good God, man! Are you drinking *again*?
Mr Tunnicliffe I've just had a telephone call from the Orkneys.
Henry That's no reason to take to the bottle.
Mr Tunnicliffe It was Mr Tipthorpe! In a telephone box! I don't know how to tell you this, but I'm afraid your brother . . . *was* killed when he fell off his tractor!

They all stare at him in astonishment

Sarah Bernard?
Mr Tunnicliffe Yes. Mr Tipthorpe was right all along.
Henry You mean he really *is* dead?
Mr Tunnicliffe Yes.
Nora Don't be daft! He's *here*!
Mr Tunnicliffe No, he isn't!
Polly But we've all seen him!
Mr Tunnicliffe You couldn't have done.
Nora Then who was it that we've all been talking to?
Polly Yes! Who was it walking about here dressed like a monk?
Mr Tunnicliffe Well, it can't have been Bernard, because he's dead.
Sarah (*her face lighting up*) Aaah . . .! I *knew* I was right . . .

They all look at her

How wonderful! So he *was* a ghost all the time . . . (*She smiles, delightedly*)
Nora Well, I don't believe in ghosts.
Henry Neither do I.

Debbie, Sally and Jackie run in from the garden

Debbie It's all right, Mrs Winthrop!
Nora What's all right?
Jackie The laundryman's gone!
Polly (*quietly*) And he's not the *only* one . . .!
Sarah Good news, girls! Bernard *was* a ghost, after all!
Jackie
Sally } (*together*) What?!
Nora If you believe that, you'll believe anything. Wait a minute! (*She turns to Henry, suspiciously*) Perhaps you've got a *better* explanation, Chief Constable?
Henry What do you mean?
Nora Well, it's funny that we've never seen you and your brother both at the same time, isn't it?

Henry That's just coincidence. Bernard was always out there when I was in here.
Nora Exactly! Not once have any of us seen you and your brother together. Isn't that right, girls?

The girls exchange looks

Polly
Debbie } *(together)* Yes!
Jackie
Sally

Sarah Yes, Henry—she's right.
Henry What are you suggesting?
Nora I'm suggesting that it must have been *you* all the time!
Henry *Me?*
Nora Dressing up and pretending to be Bernard!
Henry *(laughing)* Don't be ridiculous! Why should I do a thing like that?
Nora Well, there's no other explanation, is there? Well? What have you got to say for yourself?
Henry Now, look here, Mrs Winthrop—*I'm* the policeman—*I'll* ask the questions. (*He goes to Mr Tunnicliffe*) Give that to me! (*He snatches the bottle of whisky from him and then smiles at them all, blithely*) I shall probably see you all for dinner. (*And he walks, purposefully, to the cupboard, pulls open the door, steps inside with the bottle of whisky, and closes the door behind him*)

They are all astonished, gazing at the cupboard door. They turn and exchange incredulous looks. Then they make a concerted rush to the cupboard and try to open the door. But it is now locked from the inside

Polly He's locked the door!
Mr Tunnicliffe And taken the whisky with him . . .
Sarah Henry! Come out of there at once!
Debbie I wish I knew what was going on.
Nora He's locked himself in the cupboard!
Debbie Yes, I know that, but why?
Sarah I've never known Henry lock himself in a cupboard before . . .
Polly Do you think he'll come out?
Nora I'll soon get him out! Just you wait!

Nora marches out into the hall with the others following her. They are all talking at once

Debbie Where are we going?
Polly *I* don't know!
Sally What's she going to do?
Jackie She's going to get him out of the cupboard.
Mr Tunnicliffe I wish I knew what was going on . . .
Sarah *(as they disappear)* I can't think *why* Henry went *into* a cupboard in the first place . . .

Act II, Scene 2   67

They re-appear immediately. Nora is now carrying a small crow-bar. She makes, purposefully, for the cupboard. The others follow in her wake, chattering like magpies

Nora There! This should do the trick!
Sarah What are you going to do?
Nora You'll see!
Debbie What's she going to do?
Polly You'll see!
Mr Tunnicliffe What's she doing with a crow-bar?
Nora I'm going to get him out!
Sally With a crow-bar?
Jackie Have you got a better idea?
Sarah You're not going to break the lock, are you?
Nora (*working on the door with the crow-bar*) How else am I going to open the door?
Debbie She's not going to break the lock, is she?
Polly How else is she going to open the door?
Sarah Bernard won't be very pleased if you break the door.
Nora Don't be daft—Bernard's dead! Right—here we go—aaaaah!—*got* it!

They all gasp as the cupboard door bursts open. Everybody crowds round and peers into the cupboard. Nora barks at Henry inside

Sitting comfortably, Chief Constable?
Sarah Henry, why did you lock yourself in the cupboard?
Debbie He's sitting down in the cupboard...
Polly Funny sort of policeman who sits in a cupboard with a bottle of whisky...
Nora (*severely*) I hope you've got a good explanation for what you've been up to!
Sarah All right, Henry—you've had your little joke, dear—so now come on out!
Sally I don't think he's *going* to...!
Jackie Well, he can't stay in there!
Mr Tunnicliffe What shall we do if he won't come out?
Nora I'll *get* him out! Come on, Chief Constable, let's be having you!

Nora reaches inside the cupboard and grabs Henry's arm. She tries to pull him out of the cupboard. Sarah assists her. The others call out, encouragingly, as Nora and Sarah pull at Henry's arm. Inside the cupboard, Henry resists, determined to stay where he is. The front door slams. They all stop talking, turn and look

Bernard walks in from the front door in his cassock, and sees them

Bernard What on earth are you doing?

They cannot believe their eyes! They turn, in unison, to look at the cupboard where Henry can still be seen, Nora and Sarah clinging on to his arm. They all look back to gaze in wonder at Bernard. Sarah is delighted! Bernard smiles at them, happily

Black-out

The CURTAIN *falls*

FURNITURE AND PROPERTY LIST

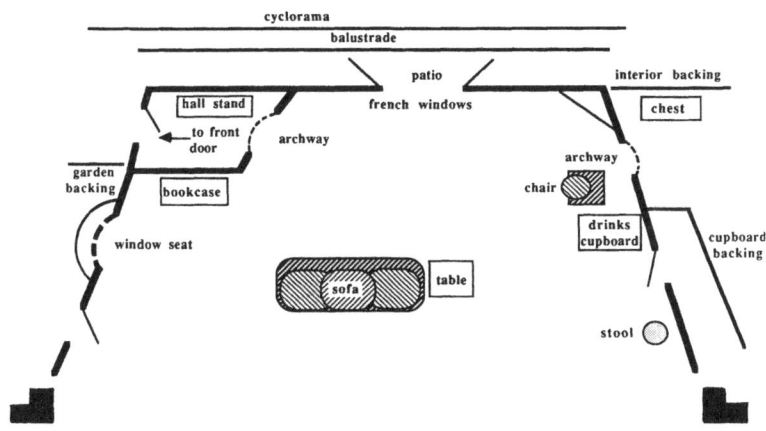

ACT I

On stage: Sofa. *On it:* cushions
Small table. *On it:* telephone, desk diary
Drinks cupboard. *On it:* table lamp. *In it:* 3 whisky glasses, 2 sherry glasses, 1 tumbler, 1 jug of water, 1 bottle of sherry, 1 bottle of whisky
Upright chair
Stool
Corner table. *On it:* table lamp
Bookcase. *On it:* table lamp. *On shelves:* books
Carpet
On walls: mirror, paintings
In passage UR*:* hallstand
Outside archway UL*:* chest
On patio: pots of flowers

Off stage: 2 suitcases, 1 grip, 2 carrier bags (full), fishing rods, keep net **(Sarah)**
2 pairs of sheets **(Nora)**
Briefcase **(Mr Tunnicliffe)**

Personal: **Nora:** whistle
Roger: hat, wrist-watch

ACT II

Scene 1

Check: Empty whisky glass
Empty sherry bottle
Bottle of whisky in cupboard

Off stage: Bread-and-cheese **(Bernard)**
Laundry basket on wheels **(Nora** and **Roger)**—required twice
Empty whisky glass **(Henry)**

Scene 2

Off stage: Shotgun **(Henry)**—required 3 times
Bottle of whisky **(Mr Tunnicliffe)**
Small crowbar **(Nora)**

LIGHTING PLOT

Property fittings required: 3 table lamps (non-practical)

Interior. A country house drawing-room. The same scene throughout

ACT I

To open: Bright spring sunshine

Cue 1   **Bernard** drinks the whisky in one   (Page 31)
Black-out

ACT II   SCENE 1

To open: Bright spring sunshine

Cue 2   **Man** appears out of laundry basket and runs out of front door.
They all react   (Page 51)
Black-out

ACT II   SCENE 2

To open: Bright spring sunshine

Cue 3   They all look at **Bernard**, then at the cupboard, then back at
Bernard. He smiles at them, happily   (Page 68)
Black-out

EFFECTS PLOT

ACT I

Cue 1	**Sarah** wanders to C *A cow moos in the garden, off*	(Page 1)
Cue 2	**Henry:** "... much use to *him* now!" *A loud blast on a whistle off* L	(Page 3)
Cue 3	**Roger** goes out into the garden, gloomily *Telephone rings*	(Page 25)
Cue 4	**Nora** opens the cupboard door *Door creak*	(Page 27)
Cue 5	**Nora** shuts the cupboard door *Door creak*	(Page 27)
Cue 6	**Henry:** "... what they're like." The cupboard door opens *Door creak*	(Page 28)
Cue 7	**Henry:** "... a bridle and saddle." The cupboard door opens *Door creak*	(Page 28)
Cue 8	As **Nora** staggers back, the cupboard door opens *Door creak*	(Page 29)
Cue 9	**Nora** goes quickly to the cupboard and opens the door *Door creak*	(Page 30)
Cue 10	**Bernard** goes towards the archway. The cupboard door opens *Door creak*	(Page 31)

ACT II

Cue 11	As **Henry** searches for the whisky bottle, the cupboard door opens *Door creak*	(Page 32)
Cue 12	**Henry** knocks on the cupboard door. It opens *Door creak*	(Page 32)
Cue 13	**Bernard** opens the cupboard door *Door creak*	(Page 35)
Cue 14	**Mr Tunnicliffe:** "... to see to the pigs ..." *Gunshot off* L	(Page 59)
Cue 15	**Mr Tunnicliffe** opens the cupboard door *Door creak*	(Page 61)

Flying Feathers

Cue 16	**Mr Tunnicliffe** closes the cupboard door *Telephone bell. It cuts out after a moment*	(Page 61)
Cue 17	**Polly** knocks on the cupboard door; it opens *Door creak*	(Page 62)
Cue 18	**Henry** opens the cupboard door *Door creak*	(Page 66)
Cue 19	**Nora** opens the cupboard door *Door creak*	(Page 67)
Cue 20	**Nora** and **Sarah** struggle with **Henry**'s arm, trying to pull him out of the cupboard *Door slams off* R	(Page 67)

MADE AND PRINTED IN GREAT BRITAIN BY
LATIMER TREND & COMPANY LTD PLYMOUTH
MADE IN ENGLAND

**Other plays by Derek Benfield
published by Samuel French Ltd**

Anyone for Breakfast?
Bedside Manners
Beyond a Joke
A Bird in the Hand
Caught on the Hop
Don't Lose the Place
Fish Out of Water
In For the Kill
Look Who's Talking!
Murder for the Asking
Off the Hook
Panic Stations
Post Horn Gallop
Running Riot
A Toe In The Water
Touch and Go
Up and Running!
Wild Goose Chase

Lightning Source UK Ltd.
Milton Keynes UK
UKOW06f0135120416

272056UK00001B/87/P